SUCCESSFUL CATERING

*Managing The Catering Operation
for Maximum Profit*

By Sony Bode

The Food Service Professional's Guide To:
Successful Catering Managing The Catering
Operation for Maximum Profit: 365 Secrets Revealed

Atlantic Publishing Group, Inc. Copyright © 2003
1210 SW 23rd Place
Ocala, Florida 34474
800-541-1336
352-622-5836 - Fax

www.atlantic-pub.com - Web site
sales@atlantic-pub.com - E-mail

SAN Number :268-1250

International Standard Book Number: 0-910627-22-3

Library of Congress Cataloging-in-Publication Data

Bode, Soni.
Successful catering-managing the catering operation for
maximum profit: 365 secrets revealed / by Soni Bode.
p. cm. -- (The Food service professionals guide to)
ISBN 0-910627-22-3 (pbk. : alk. paper)
1. Caterers and catering--Management. I. Title. II. Series.
TX921 .B58 2003
642'.4--dc21
2002013542

Printed in Canada

Book layout and design by Meg Buchner of Megadesign
www.mega-designs.com • e-mail: megadesn@mhtc.net

CONTENTS

Social caterers are one of the fastest-growing segments of the restaurant industry.

INTRODUCTION

According to the National Restaurant Association's Industry Forecast, social caterers are one of the fastest-growing segments of the restaurant industry. At present, for instance, the U.S. Yellow Pages lists in excess of 53,000 caterers. This figure includes off-premise and banquet facility caterers, not hotels. The annual sales of these 53,000 caterers are between $7 and $8 billion.

Catering has come a long way from the simple chicken and prime rib buffets of the past. "Customers today are looking for the catered experience to be more restaurant-like," says National Restaurant Association Chairman Denise Marie Fugo, who is also president and CEO of Sammy's in Cleveland. Fugo and her husband, Ralph DiOrio, started doing small, private banquets and off-premises catering in 1981. Sammy's catering eventually became so successful that Fugo closed the restaurant earlier this year to concentrate solely on catering.

While catering can be a lucrative career, let's put things in perspective. Sure, there's money to be made in the catering industry and the job satisfaction can be immense. Catering, however, is also hard work with long, unsocial hours. You also need to be able to multitask and organize your time with military precision. Often, with the best will in the world, things do go wrong!

Caterer Bev Goldberg, for instance, double-checked her master list for a cocktail party in a client's home. Linens, check. Plates, check. Glassware, check. Soft drinks, check. Garnishes, check. Hors d'oeuvres, check. Ice, check. Satisfied that everything needed for the party was ready and loaded into the van, she and two of her staff left for the event location. Upon arrival, she discovered no host and no guests! "The person who had contracted for the party had apparently forgotten and was not at home," she says with a laugh. A veteran caterer with more than 30 years' experience, Goldberg, who co-owns Artistry Catering in Chantilly, Virginia, with her son Randy, has become used to the frenetic pace and unexpected occurrences of this growing profession. "I love catering," she says. "People still think this is a glamorous job, but it's just plain hard work."

While this book can't do the work for you, it can make the work easier! Let this book come to your rescue with its tips and suggestions for the busy caterer. Get it right – the first time!

CHAPTER ONE

GETTING STARTED

How Profitable Can Catering Be?

Whether you plan to cater small intimate affairs every day, or huge extravaganzas for thousands of people once a year, the profit margin potential in the catering business is extremely high. Some caterers manage to walk away with 66 percent pre-tax profits. This figure may seem hard to believe, but when you stop and think about all the ways that caterers can keep their overhead costs at practically nothing, it becomes a more credible figure. About 70 percent of caterers report that they have been profitable each and every year of their last five years in business. Before plunging headlong into the world of catering, however, bear in mind, the best place to start is to take a look at the bottom line. Here are some rough figures to guide you:

- **You can start out at a low investment of only $1,000 if you intend to work from your own kitchen.** But, outlay can be as high as $100,000 for outfitting a professional kitchen.

- **With revenue of between $200,000 and $2,000,000,** the pre-tax profit could equal between $50,000 and $1,000,000.

- **A restaurant doing $1,000,000 in sales could earn an additional $200,000** in net profits in the first year, if it adds a catering operation, since it's fixed costs are already met.

- **The secret of increased profitability is building accounts rather than sales.** Increased volume does not always result in a monetary advantage.

Are You "Born" for Catering?

Are you an excellent cook and competent in artistic food presentation? Do you have some basic business knowledge and love working with people? Basically that's what is required to be a happy, successful caterer! Do you have the cooking skills of a good gourmet cook? Do you already have a sizable repertoire of well-tried recipes? So far, so good, but remember, not only do you have to know how to prepare all these items, you must also be able to present them in an appetizing, mouth-watering way. Here are some issues to consider before moving forward with your catering business.

- **Presentation.** You must be a master of presentation. At some venues (and especially for some clients), presentation is the be-all, end-all. When you cater a party, it is usually for a specific, special event, such as a company Christmas party or wedding. The occasion is special enough for the client to want to put on an event. The presentation of the food should reflect the importance of the occasion. Obviously, the food quality should also reflect this. While it may be true that people eat with their eyes first, they eventually eat with their mouth and taste buds!

- **Do you have planning and organizational skills?** Some areas of catering demand only a modest amount of these skills, but if you're going to do off-premise catering, you must plan and organize each event. The need for the hot food to be hot and the cold food to be icy cold aside, you'd need to make sure, for instance, that someone in your staff did not miscount the silverware, leaving you one fork short. How can you produce a single fork during the next 20 minutes when the crew's every minute is planned for the next 4 hours? While 70 percent of a typical restaurant is food-oriented with the rest going for service, organization, etc., this figure flip-flops to 30 percent in the catering business, the rest being delivery, transporting the food, lining up rental equipment and juggling personnel. In restaurants, every day is fairly similar. In the catering world, however, each day and each event is different. This makes organizational skills vital in the catering business!

- **Efficiency and ability to deal with stress.** As with any food industry business, efficiency in catering is important. You also need to ask yourself if you can work well under pressure. Because each event is unique, catering can be more stressful than many professions. It's not that most professions do not demand these skills, but in catering, you not only have to deal with the stress, you also have to make sure that your customer never sees the stress. You need to be cool and smile, no matter how you may feel inwardly. Don't get too stressed out about stress, however. Once the guests taste your food and start "ooh-ah-ing" at your presentation, you can relax.

- **Expect the unexpected.** Expect problems to happen and be ready to solve them, quickly and inventively. You need to have good crisis-management and problem-solving skills in catering. With off-premise catering, for example, you'll have to deal with event site problems, serving the food at unfamiliar locations and trying to find delivery entrances and parking spots. Face the truth! With catering you have to learn to live with the fact that you're in the limelight, where there is so much opportunity for errors.

- **Confidence and communication.** Are you out-going? Remember that it is YOU and not your company that is being hired. You must PERSONALLY impress your client or else you don't have a deal!

Make your first impression your best impression. If you have almost all the above-mentioned assets and lack on this one, take some evening courses on public speaking, for instance, or just rent a couple of books and audio guides offering techniques on better communication and presentation skills.

- **You are the salesperson.** Eventually, you may have salespeople working for you, but when you start out in catering, you'll be your own sales person. You'll be dealing with corporate executives, party planners and nervous brides. You'll need to convince these prospective clients that you'll not only provide a memorable feast, but that it'll be there on time, presented attractively and served unobtrusively! You'll also need to come up with ways in which to attract business, and retain it, once you've been hired.

- **Sidelines.** Don't limit your options – be creative! There are a number of sidelines that naturally spring from the catering business. For example, you can act as a coordinator for flowers, ice sculptures, photography, party locations or themes. At the same time, remember that if people wanted to stick to a set menu, they could go to a restaurant, so be flexible. In many catering establishments, this may not be an option. In hotel catering, for instance, there is not much room for flexibility. If you are marketing to smaller events, or have the resources to be flexible, let your menu suggestions be just that. These can be a starting point, but let the client be your guide. Don't miss opportunities to turn a modest "do" into a major profit-making event. Also, don't hesitate when you see an opportunity to "bump-up" the bottom line of an event. You may be able to turn a barbecue into a Hawaiian luau complete with a roast pig. Make sure that every event is a party to remember.

Catering Potential in Your Community

A careful analysis of your potential customer base is vital. This task goes beyond estimating whether you have enough events to cater for in your area and whether you have the necessary drive and flair to stay the course. You need to explore the competition. Find out who your competitors are and what market share they already cover. Without this information, you simply cannot be successful in the catering business. Take a long, hard look at the competition. Here are some suggestions:

- **Contact your local Bureau of Vital Statistics and/or Bureau of Records.** Find out the number of births, marriages and deaths in your community. This will help to indicate to you the potential number of events catered in your area.

- **Check the local newspapers' society columns.** This resource will provide you with wedding announcements and other social events in your area. It will also provide you with some of the names of key players in the social world. Jot down these names and add them to your list of marketing contacts.

- **Organizations.** Check with some non-profit organizations and fraternal clubs, as well as your area's clubs, churches, etc. Ask them how many catered events took place in their function rooms.

- **Gather the necessary data.** Don't forget to ask for relevant data from the local chamber of commerce and your local Small Business Administration office. You can find contact information for local small business associations at www.sba.gov.

- **Yellow Pages.** Check your local Yellow Pages to get a sense of the competition. Keep in mind, however, that many small operations probably are not listed, due to the expense. You should also do a Web search to find area competition; these days, many, if not most, businesses have a Web page. When assessing the competition, you will want to find out how many catering operations exist, in your locality and what their main target audiences are.

Choosing a Name

If choosing a name for the newborn baby is fun, it's even more so to coin a name for your new business. Your business name is your identity. It shows your clients your idea about where you position yourself in the world of catering. Here are a few guidelines:

- **Experiment.** Don't be afraid to experiment with names by choosing, for instance, the one that is most likely to become imprinted in the prospective client's mind, "Beyond A Mouthful," maybe? Or, for example, you could name your business after your services' characteristics, perhaps "The Floating Feast." Alternatively your name may represent a personal touch, such as "Catering by Daphne." If you are a known persona or chef within your community, naming your business after yourself could help create extra business opportunities.

- **Let your name sell your services.** Remember that your name must serve first and foremost as a selling tool. Be wise. Find a name that reflects the mouth-watering food you're capable of preparing for your guests.

- **Choose a name that is pronounceable.** Usually, short business names are best because they are more likely to be remembered by potential customers. You could also use alliteration or a play-on-words, for the same affect. A customer is likely to remember "The Moveable Feast," because it is based on the name of a novel by Ernest Hemingway. "A

Forkable Feast" is also memorable because of the alliteration in the phrase. Both of these names suggest the kind of catering provided by the establishment. "A Moveable Feast," for instance, would specialize in off-premises catering; "A Forkable Feast" may specialize in tapas or cocktail receptions.

- **Consider alphabetical order.** This is especially important if you intend to rely upon sales generated from the phone book. We've all seen the "AAA" listing for everything from exterminators to event planners. People do tend to pick from the top of the list when faced with many choices. So, having your business start with the letter "A" is a good idea.

- **Avoid duplication.** Make sure you register the chosen name with the state under which you're going to do business. The name will become a public record. First, establish that the name that you've selected is not being used by anyone else. Fill out the forms and pay a fee to record it. You may also need to run a fictitious business name statement four times in a local, legally qualified (weekly) newspaper. If no one protests, the name is officially yours.

- **Contact the Secretary of State in your home state.** Check for name availability and register your name with the Secretary of State. Many states have their services available online.

- **Legal requirements.** When setting up a catering business, there are certain legal issues that you simply cannot avoid. Come to grips with these few basics. You'll need to know the following:

- **Business entity formation.** Seek legal advice in developing your business organization. In most cases you will want to organize as a corporation, either an S or the new LLC, or limited liability corporation. ncorporating gives you maximum protection

15

against creditors and the possibility of a client lawsuit, but you should check with your attorney and accountant about other legal and tax issues that will affect you as a corporation.

- **Get a federal tax number for your business** (also called an EIN - Employer Identification Number). Fill out the IRS Form SS-4. You'll need it in order to pay the following federal taxes: income taxes withheld from employee wages, employer/employee Social Security tax (FICA), employer/employee Medicare tax (MICA) and federal unemployment tax (FUTA). For more information on business taxes, visit the IRS's Web site at www.irs.gov.

- **Local and state sales taxes.** Contact your municipality/state department/division of revenue for the requirements. You can also find some state tax information at www.bizsites.com/webxtras/location consultants.html. This site houses information on corporate tax rates in each state and provides a state tax comparison.

- **Zoning.** Beware of zoning restrictions. Local ordinances may impose restrictions on where you locate your business. Your physical plant is subject to proper clearances from the local zoning board. You'll need a Certificate of Use and Occupancy from your municipality before the business can be conducted legally. Off-premises caterers who construct a new facility or convert an existing building, previously used for other purposes, will have to check zoning regulations carefully. To operate a business on land not zoned for that purpose, a conditional-use permit may be required.

- **A license from the local health board is mandatory.** Once your commercial kitchen has passed the inspection based on health department regulations, you can operate legitimately from your kitchen. Your establishment might be considered a commissary, restaurant or food-processing plant. You're better off applying for the type of license that will allow maximum flexibility, permitting broader privileges such as retailing, for example.

• **Obtain a resale license.** This is necessary to prove to your suppliers that you are in legitimate business and have the right to purchase from a wholesaler. Since you are reselling, you will not be charged sales tax on products that are resold in your business.

• **U.S. Small Business Administration (SBA).** This is a great resource for people starting and operating a business. You can find this organization at www.sba.gov. The SBA offers online training and workbooks. You can also find links to local SBA offices.

• **Service Corps of Retired Executives (SCORE).** This organization is also a great business resource. SCORE is comprised of volunteers who help new business owners with the myriad of questions they have. Find them online at www.score.org. You can find local offices, business counseling and "how to" articles, among other things, on this Web site.

Insurance Requirements

You can't afford to buy insurance and pay premiums? Well, in fact, you can't afford not to! Don't make the mistake of not having the following types of insurances:

• **Product liability insurance.** Just imagine: a foreign object is found in your customers' food. You could be sued! Product liability insurance was designed to protect in just such an instance. What if a bride wants you to serve a wedding cake made by her best friend? This friend is making the cake in her home, but she has no product insurance, no licenses and no permit from the Board of Health. Further, you have no control over how the product was made. In this case, you should explain to the bride that she will need to sign a liability waiver with your company. By signing this waiver, the bride gives up her rights and her guests' rights to any legal action against you in the event of food contamination that might be caused by the product you did not make. Of course, she could always just buy the cake from you and save herself the trouble!

- **Liability insurance.** A potential client, while touring on the caterer's premises, slips and falls on a wet floor and becomes injured. An employee, while serving hot gravy, spills it, damaging the guest's evening gown and severely burning her leg. Liability insurance is the type of insurance that would protect you against all the above-mentioned claims. Rather than insuring you against problems with the food, this type of insurance is meant for harm caused because of equipment and employees.

- **Fire insurance.** Comprehensive coverage including, for example, wind, storm, smoke, explosion, malicious mischief, etc., is recommended.

- **Auto insurance.** Be aware that even when an employee uses his or her own car on your behalf, you could be legally liable for an accident. The caterer may not have directed the employee's action, but if an accident occurs while that employee is on a business trip on behalf of the owner, the caterer can still be named in a lawsuit. Auto insurance helps protect against such losses. Low-cost fleet policies are available when insuring five or more vehicles. Check with your insurance agents for other discounts they may offer.

- **Workers' compensation insurance.** Avoid the risk of employee lawsuits – provide workers' compensation insurance. Most states require employers to carry workers' compensation insurance, if they have one or more workers. Catering is a high-risk business and chances of accidents are greater than in many other businesses. Providing a safe place to work, safe tools, training and warning employees of existing dangers are great policies and a good start to keeping your employees safe. But, you'll also need to take out insurance protection. Check on the Web to locate your state workers' compensation bureau.

- **Employee Benefit Insurance Coverage.** Insurance benefits for employees, such as health, dental and disability insurance, can be very expensive for a small business. Regardless, you may want to consider offering basic health insurance, group life insurance, disability insurance and retirement coverage. By offering your employees these benefits, you will gain more loyal, reliable employees and it may be worth the cost. Check with your local Yellow Pages for insurance agents. Make sure you get several quotes before making a decision!

There are many aspects to catering.

CHAPTER TWO

TYPES OF CATERING

The Pros and Cons of Home-Based Catering

By definition, catering is the act of providing food and services. Today, catering involves so many aspects, whether the enterprise is home-based or a large-scale operation. In many instances, home-based caterers tend to have limited experience, smaller insurance policies and less knowledge about proper sanitation. In fact, these caterers are sometimes viewed as unfair competition to a licensed caterer, because the home-based caterer does not incur the same expenses, has low overhead and is able to price at lower cost-per-plate than the licensed caterer. If you're thinking of testing the waters with a small-scale, home-based business, you'll need to consider the following issues:

- **Health department regulations.** Let's say you've decided to set up your catering service in your own home, using a spare bedroom as your office. If you intend to use your own kitchen, you'll first need to check out the health department regulations that govern the catering trade. Make no assumptions. If you overlook the smallest detail regarding health regulations, you could be out of business before you know it! You can be certain the first job you take from a licensed caterer will be your last if you are not properly licensed.

- **Consider renting a kitchen.** Perhaps rent a kitchen in a restaurant, school or church on an "as-needed" basis. One of the main advantages is that you won't need to employ any full-time employees and there's a whole army of part-timers out there, willing to work when you need them.

- **Think about limiting your events to those in equipped kitchens.** If you cannot find a kitchen to work in, consider limiting your events to those in venues that come equipped. While it may cramp your style in the beginning, it could provide you with the capital you need to purchase a site and equipment at a later date.

- **Small business incubators.** Many areas have small business incubator programs. These programs provide entrepreneurs with networking opportunities and resources. Some of these incubators have kitchens available for a rental fee. To find out more about the business incubator program, you can log on to www.nbia.org.

- **Tableware and the home-based setup.** Even if you decide to use your own kitchen and cooking equipment, you may be better off renting the necessary tableware, etc. In the catering trade, there are very few items you can't rent for the day, including china, flatware, glasses, tents and more. Places to rent this type of equipment will be listed under "party supplies" in your local Yellow Pages.

- **Personal touches.** Just because you're home-based, doesn't mean that you can't provide the same wide range of products and services as a large-scale caterer. In fact, smaller operations are better able to add those individual touches to their presentation and services. In addition to the food, think about including table and chair setup, napkins and eating utensils and even complete cleanup services.

- **Attentive service is just as important as delicious food.** Don't take on jobs that are too big for your operation. The quality of service will suffer and so will your reputation. A typical home-based business is better off concentrating on food quality and personal service rather than quantity. Aim for jobs that involve between 20-100 guests. This size of event should not overtax you and your staff. If you take on a larger party, think about using some convenience products rather than trying to make every menu item from scratch. For example, you may want to buy homemade ravioli from the store that makes these, rather than making them yourself. You also have the option of hiring additional staff, if needed.

• **Pay attention to your menu choices if you take on a large event.** If you're doing a cocktail reception for 20, it's easy to make such items as shrimp mousse on cucumber rounds, stuffed with grape leaves and raspberry and brie tartlets. If you're catering a reception for 100, however, you'll want to stay away from labor-intensive pick-up appetizers. For this size party, you should consider serving dips such as humus or guacamole and have displays such as a cheese board or shrimp cocktail.

• **Home chefs.** A trend that has gained popularity in the last several years is the home-chef business. A home chef goes to a customer's house and cooks enough meals for a week or two weeks and stores these for the customer to eat, at their convenience. The home chef brings all the necessary equipment, does the menu planning and grocery shopping. This option eliminates the need for a commercial kitchen and allows you to cook a greater variety of items than if you were catering large events. To find out more about home chefs, visit the United States Personal Chef Association's Web site at www.uspca.com.

Off-Premises Catering

Off-premise catering has certain advantages over on-premise catering. In fact, all you need is a kitchen facility, coined as a commissary, that will be used exclusively for preparation of foods to be served at other locations. The experience can also be more exciting if you're the type of caterer who enjoys the challenge of working in unusual and unique locations and dealing with new people who you'll probably never meet again. Mobile catering is a very interesting facet of the catering segment. A few companies specialize in feeding forest firefighters, disaster relief workers, construction site workers, people taking camping trips or excursions, etc. They develop a seasonal menu and a picnic-table concept on the back of properly equipped truck; usually they furnish hot or cold sandwiches, beverages, soup, coffee, bagels, burritos and much more. There are several important considerations you'll need to bear in mind when it comes to running an off-premise catering business:

- **Teamwork.** Build a strong team with strong leadership. Remember, the teamwork required in an off-premise-type catering operation can make your company stronger. Your staff will learn to handle just about everything that can go wrong and, most importantly, you'll have the potential to make six-figure incomes each year! Teamwork is critical.

- **Off-premise catering is both an art and a science.** Create foods AND moods, while measuring money, manpower and material. Remember, you only have one chance to do it right, since many catering events happen only once in a person's (that is your client's) lifetime. If you fail to satisfy the client, you will not be given another chance.

- **Subcontractors.** As the overall operating costs for off-premise catering are generally lower than for on-premises catering, you may find it within your budget to engage subcontractors for certain aspects of the event; e.g., floral design, music and entertainment. This can often prove more cost-effective than doing it yourself. Many cities have agencies that provide these services. Check the Yellow Pages for such agencies under "entertainment." You should also use your networking skills in this area. Do you know other caterers? Whom do they use for flowers? Maybe you are linked to the music segment of your town. If so, you already have a stable of musicians that you can contact.

- **Can you cater for different numbers of people at various locations?** You may be able to handle a hundred people in your facility, but can you do the same thing at the church facility where you have never been before? Make sure that you visit a site before getting into a contract for an event.

- **Five keys to success.** Here are five important things to look out for when engaging in off-premise catering:

- **Be ready for surprises**. There are literally thousands of potentially dangerous exploding mines that can ruin an otherwise successful affair. For example, you are catering a bar mitzvah. Your cook does not realize there is a difference between kosher hot dogs and regular hot dogs. But, you don't realize this until you are unpacking at the event site. Now what do you do! Always have a Plan B. In the case of the non-kosher hot dogs, Plan B was to send a runner to the nearest grocery and purchase the promised product!

- **Be prepared.** You'll need to be organized. Plan ahead. Visualize in advance all of the aspects of a catered event. As a catering professional, you'll find that you make many lists. Be sure to check these lists four times before an event – and then check them again! Have someone else check them as well; they may catch something you missed. A catering worksheet is available for downloading on www.restaurantbeast.com.

- **Do a site visit.** If you're catering for an event off-premises, be sure you visit the site! This should be done during the early planning stages. You should visit the site again as the day approaches. Compare what you see with your lists and make

25

sure you bring everything you need to make the event a success.

- **Be smart.** Understand that you can only be successful in off-site catering by running your company from the center of the action and for that, you need to be involved in all of the details of the business. Ask for feedback from the client and guests. Oversee the catering staff to make sure that they are performing to required standards. This also means jumping in and helping out when a table needs to be bused or coffees need to be refilled.

- **Don't act like an amateur.** Be professional, courteous, ethical and customer-focused in your dealings with clients. Maintain truth in your menu. Do not engage in misleading advertising or unexpected and unjustified last-minute add-ons to the party price. Also, do not underbid a competitor when the client discloses your competitor's price.

- **Separate yourself from the competition.** Do not copy the competition. Try to do it by offering a unique menu, a unique service, or, perhaps, a unique location. What do you do best? Focus on this rather than trying to be something else. If you make exceptional vegetarian dishes, for example, be sure to include at least one on your menus whenever possible.

- **Keep cool.** The customer is screaming, the brioche is burning and one of your staff members just cut himself. The result: stress. Learn how to deal with it! A step in the right direction is to manage your time effectively. Set realistic goals – for a lifetime, for five years, for each year, month, week and for each day.

On-Premises Catering

On-premises catering is defined as catering for an event held on the physical premises of the facility that is organizing the function. It is estimated that on-premise catering accounts for about two-thirds of all catering sales in the U.S. On-premise catering operations range from large profit-oriented and "not-for-profit" operations to smaller, start-up enterprises! If you're a small-scale on-premise caterer, however, do not despair. There is a growing demand for your types of services. After all, small on-premises caterers have the advantage of greater flexibility when it comes to price structures – owing to lower overhead expenses. The following tips apply to all on-premises catering operations – however big or small:

- **Competition.** Focus on the competition at all times, not just at the planning stage. Keep up to date. Who, for instance, are the major players in your sector of the industry? Visit their establishments and listen to their clientele.

- **Specialize.** If you're looking for a niche in the on-premises catering business, explore the possibilities of wedding and convention catering. Weddings, in particular, can yield high profits, largely because of all the extra purchases that can be incorporated into a single event. A word of caution – to ensure first-class reliability and dependability, include a bridal consultant in your staff. You'll be in a better position to understand, for example, the subtleties of cultural differences and requirements that can make all the difference between success and failure in the wedding catering industry. You should also become familiar with the rituals of traditional weddings and the types of concerns bridal couples and their parents will have. There are many Web sites devoted to people planning weddings. Visit any of these to see the types of concerns couples will have. One such Web site is at www.usabride.com.

- **Streamline.** Make sure that the layout of your premises works with you, rather than against you. The convenience factor is important when you're working under pressure. Remember, the distinct advantage of catering on-premises is that everything can be positioned pretty much within reach. If, for example, a customer receives a steak they do not like, another one can be prepared without serious difficulty. This may not be an alternative when serving at an off-premises location.

- **Comfort.** With on-premise catering, you need to make sure you know how many people can be comfortably seated in your facility. Are you able to provide entertainment? Also, can you prepare a wide variety of menu items at the last minute?

- **Clubs.** If you run a private club, promote your catering services amongst your members. Offer special deals for private parties and celebrations. Country clubs are better off concentrating on catering for weddings, dances, etc. City clubs are advised to target the business sector. Consider specializing in catering for corporate meetings, board luncheons, civic events, etc. There are many marketing opportunities to help develop this clientele. Join your local chamber of commerce and become involved in your city. These alliances will provide you with networking opportunities and new business!

The Best of Both Worlds

Many restaurateurs cater on-premise special events and also pursue off-premise opportunities. Dual restaurant catering may be advantageous because restaurateurs have invested in professional production equipment. By serving both markets, you can lower the overall fixed costs of your operation while increasing, incrementally, gross sales. This increase in sales can be achieved without having to spend money on expanding the dining room or kitchen area. When in the pursuit of both types of business, aim to achieve the following:

- **Maximize on flexibility.** Take advantage of the flexibility offered by a combination of on-premises/off-premises catering. By blending both types of catering, dual restaurant-catering operations enjoy the freedom to prepare their foods within their own facility, while at the same time employing outside labor.

- **Maximize on expertise.** Because of the flexibility offered by dual catering operations, you can draw on a greater pool of specialist expertise. This means that you will be in greater demand for a wider range of significant events.

- **Maximize on exclusivity.** Define your exclusive target market. Determine, in advance, the specific clientele for your business. Securing exclusive clients is a definite advantage for a caterer; it will give you a strategic advantage over many other caterers in the market. Work towards exceeding your client's needs. It will bring you recognition and market dominance, in an exclusive area of the catering trade.

- **Develop a seasonal niche.** The dual caterer should be aware of certain special annual events. These events involve preparation of the food on your own premises, while serving off-premises. The advantage of off-premises catering is that you can serve a greater number of people than at your own premises. Understand, however, that the design of your kitchen will determine your capacity to cater off-premises.

A written contract

is essential.

CHAPTER THREE

WRITING A CONTRACT

Contracts and Deposits

There is good reason that an entire section has been dedicated to the issue of contracts. Without a contract, you'd find yourself without a leg to stand on when attempting to collect from a non-paying customer. Simply put: It is a "must"; a contract is a binding agreement between two parties; the caterer is obligated to provide the food and service stated and the other party, your client, is obligated to pay for the food and service. You cannot afford to skip the following points:

- **Agreements should be committed in writing.** In many states, only contracts in writing are enforceable. A written contract will encourage your client to ask for additional services to be provided, during the initial phase of your negotiations. Don't let a client take advantage of you, your business or your resources.

- **Ask for a deposit.** Ask for a deposit. Ask for a deposit! Always ask for a deposit upfront. Any time you do not receive a deposit, you are in danger of cancellation, even at the last minute. Deposit policies ary; some caterers get one-third when booking, one-third one month in advance and the remainder on the day of the event. Alternatively, a caterer may receive 10 percent on booking, up to 50 percent a month in advance and the balance on the day of the event.

- **Tone.** Don't forget: if the tone of your contract is too aggressive, you're likely to alienate your clients. If it's too soft, you could end up the loser. Think carefully about the tone of your contract. You can still convey the same information, but without being antagonistic. Templates and examples of contracts can be found at www.catersource.com and www.restaurantbeast.com.

- **Take extra care with catering contracts for weddings.** Obtain as many signatures as possible on the contract, from both sides of the family. Better safe than sorry, should the need for legal collection procedures arise.

Determining Charges

There are many ways to price a catered event, simply because there are so many factors to be taken into account. First, you'll need to calculate all the direct costs of the event – the food and labor costs – as well as the indirect ones, such as licenses, office supplies, marketing and advertising. These calculations need to be made before approaching the client with a written contract to accept the cost for your food and services. Here are a few guidelines to help you determine the charges for your catering services:

- **Determine your pitch.** In order to come up with a realistic and profitable rate, you'll need to consider the rates for your area, the type of party being catered for, whether you hope to get repeat business from the client and the buoyancy of your current business.

- **Next, analyze your competitors.** Understandably, it's not as simple as adopting the competitors' prices; however, you'll get an idea of the cost range within which you can work. You can gather this information, incognito, by calling competitors and asking them to send you some sample menus. Many caterers also have Web sites, so you may be able to find this information online as well.

- **Use your income statement (profit & loss).** It's a good idea to calculate an income statement for each party or function as if it was a one-time event. This way you can calculate a profit margin that guarantees financial success for every event.

- **Build in a 10-percent buffer.** Build in a buffer of 10 percent to cover for the possibility of food being damaged or wasted, as well as for the extra quantity that may be needed for additional guests. Now, once the food cost is determined, you can develop a factor to get the function charge.

- **Food cost.** In general, caterers (and restaurateurs) seek a food cost that is approximately 30 percent of their revenue. To determine the food cost of a particular menu item, you'll need to cost out the recipe. Usually, food cost is expressed as a percentage of the menu price or the overall sales. Food cost of a specific menu item is figured by dividing the cost of the ingredients for the item by the menu price. This figure is usually expressed as a percentage. Let's say one of your menu items is a pan-seared duck breast with an orange-loganberry sauce. First, you must look at your invoices and determine the cost of the ingredients for a single serving. This cost needs to include the duck, the ingredients and any side dishes and garnishes. Your math shows the item cost you $4.20. Now, if you want to maintain a food cost of 30 percent, where do you need to price the duck breast?

$4.20 (ingredient food cost) ÷ 0.30 (30% food cost) = $14.00 (selling price).

To determine the revenue you can make from an item, you'll want to look at the cost, the menu price and your sales history. If you divide the total income into the total cost of the item, you can determine food cost for a particular event. For example, if you cater an event for 200 people:

$840 (cost of $4.20 multiplied by 200) ÷ $2800 (sold 200 at $14.00) = 30%.

- **Labor costs.** Don't forget to add labor into your menu price calculations. Catering kitchen staff members are usually treated as regular employees; servers are often hired as independent contracts. The labor for both these categories needs to go into your price calculations. If that party for 200 people took your cook 10 hours to prepare, at an hourly rate of $10, you need to add $100 to the total. Likewise, if it took four servers 4 hours each to serve the meal, you need to add their fee. (Generally, servers are paid by 4-hour periods. Currently the going rate is between $75 and $95 for 4 hours):

4 servers $75 (4 hours each) = $300.

Full-service food service establishments try to keep labor costs below 30 percent as well. So, if we add the labor cost to the food cost, let's see what our new menu price would be. First divide the labor by 200 to come up with a per-person labor cost:

$300 (servers) + $100 (cook) = $400 ÷ 200 = $2.

Our total cost (excluding overhead) is $6.20, so if we charge $14, we will see a profit (excluding overhead) of 44 percent.

$6.20 ÷ $14 = 44%.

- **Overhead costs.** Overhead costs are particular to each operation, so we will not offer an example of these. But, don't forget to add them into the equation when you are determining menu prices!

Determining Function Space

If you are doing on-site or off-site catering, you will need to be able to determine the number of people that can be comfortably seated in the room. Each setup also presents different challenges to the caterer serving the function. There are several normal room setups used for functions. Here's what you need to know about determining function space:

- **Get familiar with room setup lingo.**

- **Banquet.** This setup is used for weddings as well as most dinner and lunch events. It includes "rounds," which are round banquet tables that usually seat eight or ten people.

- **Classroom style.** This setup is used for seminars and similar events. It is set up like a classroom, with 6- or 8-foot long banquet tables, facing the front of the room.

- **Boardroom style.** This setup is often used for smaller meetings such as board or director meetings. The room is usually set up with the participants around one large table.

- **Theater style.** This setup is exactly the same as classroom style, but there are no tables, only chairs.

- **Carry a calculator.** This is especially important if you do off-premises catering. You'll need to do some math to figure out how each space that you look at can accommodate the event you are discussing with customers. For example, if you are talking with a bride about a reception for 200 in a ballroom with 4,000 square feet, you have to determine how many banquet rounds you can fit into the room. You also need to account for space for the buffet, the wedding cake table, the DJ or band, a dance floor and a bar.

- **On-premises catering.** If you only do on-site catering, once you know the size of your facility and how many people will fit into the various setups, all you have to do is keep a binder containing this information. Keep this binder handy when meeting with potential clients so that you can show the client different setups and options for the use of your facility's space.

- **Software.** Most of the larger hotels use software that can determine room capacities. You can find event planning software at www.certain.com. Their program Event Planner Plus costs around $500. Along with creating room layouts, this software will track attendance, create a budget, track travel and lodging arrangements, compare vendor quotes and create task lists. Another Web site, www.catermate.com, also offers software that can be used for room layouts, client tracking, event sheets and more.

- **Accessories.** Often the food is only part of an event. You'll need to find out if this is the case. Does this event include a presentation or seminar? Talk to the client about additional needs such as a podium, a riser for speakers, flags easels, slide projectors, lighting, head tables and background music.

Basic Contract Stipulations and Considerations

The following list of stipulations and considerations is intended as a guideline only. It is by no means exclusive. The intention is to draw your attention to a few basic requirements. When developing your catering contract template, bear in mind the following:

- **Personal details.** When composing a contract, first include your name, address, phone and fax numbers. Next, enter the client's name, address, phone and fax numbers.

- **Dates and times.** After indicating the date of the contract, state the day and date of the event to be catered, as well as the starting and ending times for the party. The exact amount of time allocated to each activity is especially important; if the caterer runs into overtime, an overtime charge should be applied against the client.

- **Make sure to nail down the minimum number of guests.** Establish, as closely as possible, the exact number of people to be catered. If this isn't possible, ascertain at least the minimum number of guests. You need to build in a clause that permits you to raise the price per person, should you end up catering for less than the estimated minimum number of guests. Also include a clause indicating that you need final numbers by a particular date. Most caterers ask the client to give them a final guest count three days before the event. This allows the caterer an appropriate amount of time to shop and prepare the correct amount of food.

- **Determine a method for tracking the number of guests.** Some common methods for tracking numbers include tickets, plates issued, bundled/rolled silverware with a napkin issued and by a turnstile. Today, many events are preceded by invitations that request an RSVP. The RSVP reply allows you to have a more accurate guest count and can greatly help the caterer on what to anticipate. If you have an event that is not RSVP, you still need to know how much food to prepare.

- **So, how do you determine how many guests will show up?** Here's an easy formula:

  Number of guests invited x .66 x 1.15 = number of guests to anticipate. For example: 300 invited guests x .66 x 1.15 = 228 anticipated guests. The .66

accounts for the number of no-shows, and the 1.15 accounts for the uninvited guests that will arrive.

- **Guard your reputation.** Regardless of how you arrive at your number, remember that if the caterer runs out of food, it's the caterer's reputation at stake. The guests won't know that the host under-estimated the count, nor will they care. They'll just know that they're hungry, there's no food left and it's the caterer's fault! Overcome this dilemma by covering your costs for producing extra food. Let the clients know that they're always welcome to take home any unused portions. Generally, caterers have a guarantee number as well as a real number for the guest count. This guarantee usually runs between 3 and 5 percent of the total. In other words, if the event is set for 200 people, the caterer will prepare food for 206 as their guarantee number is 3 percent.

- **Include a section in the contract that details the menu to be served.** Nothing should be left out and nothing should be assumed! If you need to make major changes to the menu, (and you probably will!), draw up a new contract.

- **Event price.** An event price is established at the same time as the client is shopping for a caterer. The contract must state that the price is an approximate estimate only. Include a clause that permits the caterer to adjust the price based on unforeseen conditions. Large events are booked approximately 6 months in advance. Smaller events may occur, at much shorter notice. Most caterers have guidelines for the latest date that they can accept a job. For instance, a caterer may stipulate that he or she will book up to 3 days prior to the event.

- **Payment policy.** According to the schedule agreed, include a clause stating unequivocally the method and time frame for the payments. In general, the larger and more expensive the event, the larger the deposit.

- **Staffing.** Include a section in the clause that states the number of staff to be provided, the hours they will work, as well as applicable charges for their services.

- **Define your policies regarding leftover food and alcohol.** Often, this may be determined partially by the event. If you are catering a 40-person dinner party at a client's house, you're likely to box and leave the leftovers. If, on the other hand, you're catering a wedding reception for 150 guests at a rented hall, you'll probably take the leftovers back with you and divide amongst the staff. (All the leftovers, that is except for a to-go plate for the bride and groom.) This is a nice gesture, since the bride and groom rarely get to eat! You should also state your policy on serving alcoholic beverages to minors or those people who become intoxicated.

- **Cancellation/refund policy.** Discussed in detail in the following section, your policy regarding cancellations and refunds must be clearly spelled out in the contract.

- **Caterer and client signatures.** Don't forget - without the necessary signatures, the contract is not legally binding.

Cancellations and Refunds

Most caterers, at the time of a cancellation, will have some kind of deposit from their clients. Now, should you refund some, all, or none of the deposit? In general, there are no clear-cut answers to this and you should determine it on a case-by-case basis. The timing of cancellations is crucial in determining your policy. If someone cancels months before the event, you can probably re-book the date. If, however, the client cancels a week ahead of time, you may not be able to re-book and you might easily lose deposits you made on rentals, or money you have **39** already spent on food purchases. When deciding upon the fairest course of action, consider the following issues:

- **Hotels often have a step refund policy.** For example, if a client cancels three months before the event, the hotel will refund the entire deposit. If the event is cancelled a month before, the hotel will refund 50 percent and if the booking is cancelled a week to a month in advance, 35 percent of the deposit will be refunded. If the event is canceled within the week of its occurrence, no refund is issued. This type of step policy helps to offset some of the costs that the caterer may have already absorbed.

- **If the client cancels at least a month before the scheduled event, you may want to:**

- **Refund the full deposit.** In fact, you can very well use this policy as a selling point when a client is trying to decide between you and another caterer, for example.

- **If the event is scheduled within a month of cancellation, discuss the matter with the client personally.**

- **If the cancellation happened at the last minute** due to a tragedy involving one of the principals, for instance, it is best to wait a period of time before getting the client to discuss refunds.

- **When you're not sure how to handle the cancellation, postpone your decision;** tell the client that you have to check with the manager to see how much money and time has already been invested. This will give you time to calculate a reasonable amount to pay for costs you've already made. Refund the rest.

Sample Contract Agreement

The following sample may help you draw up your own catering contract agreement. Use it as a guideline only; consider obtaining professional legal advice:

DAPHNE'S CATERING

In consideration of the services to be performed by [insert Caterer's name here] ("Caterer") for the benefit of [insert Client's name here] ("Client") at the event scheduled for [insert event's date here], 200_, ("Event") as set forth in the attached invoice, Client agrees to the following terms and conditions:

1. In arranging for private functions, the attendance must be specified and communicated to the Caterer by 12:00 p.m., at least seven (7) days in advance. If the actual number in attendance is greater than the amount confirmed, Caterer cannot guarantee that adequate food will be available for all persons attending. If the actual number is more than 20 percent less than the number confirmed, Caterer reserves the right to increase the price per person.

2. In order to reserve the date of the Event, the Client must deliver a copy of this Agreement to Caterer along with a Deposit ("Deposit") of 50 percent of the invoice amount. The balance is due and payable no later than the day on which the event is scheduled to be held.

3. If the Client fails to make any payments when due, this Agreement may be cancelled or rejected by Caterer, and the Client agrees that Caterer shall not thereafter be obligated to provide any services hereunder. Client agrees that Caterer may retain 50 percent of the Deposit, as liquidated damages and not as a penalty, which represents a reasonable estimation of fair compensation to Caterer for damages incurred by Caterer resulting from such failure to pay or cancellation by the Client.

4. Menu requirements are to be followed as discussed and agreed

upon with Client. All food and beverage is subject to __ percent sales tax and __ percent service charge. No beverages of any kind will be permitted to be brought onto the premise by the Client or any of the guests or invitees from the outside without the special permission of the Caterer, and the Caterer reserves the right to make a charge for the service of such beverages.

5. Performance of this Agreement is contingent upon the ability of the Caterer to complete the same and is subject to labor troubles, disputes or strikes, accidents, government requisitions, restrictions upon travel, transportation, food, beverages or supplies and other causes beyond the Caterer's control that may prevent or interfere with performance. In no event shall Caterer be liable for the loss of profit, or for other similar or dissimilar collateral or consequential damages, whether on breach of contract, warranty, or otherwise.

6. Client agrees to indemnify and hold harmless Caterer for any damage, theft or loss of Caterer's property (including without limitation, equipment, plates, utensils and motor vehicles) occurring at the Event that is caused by persons attending the Event.

CHAPTER FOUR

STAFFING & PERSONNEL

Grasp the Basics About Staffing and Personnel

What is one of the biggest challenges you face as a caterer? Labor issues! These concerns include hiring chefs, kitchen personnel, service staff (both full- and part-time) and sales staff. With our economy's current low rate of unemployment, this response comes as no surprise. A recent report published by the National Restaurant Association, www.restaurant.org, mirrored the concerns of the operators on this point. Staffing for catering is an ongoing activity because your requirements fluctuate widely. Is it a very difficult task to find employees for your catering needs? Well, yes and no. While it seems that there are a lot of people out there willing to work for you on a per-hour basis, it is by no means an easy job to cultivate potential employees. Be aware that many staff members will be variable cost employees who tend to work for other caterers as well. They may well leave you on short notice for full-time, permanent employment elsewhere. It is a fact that the labor shortage frustrates your efforts to build and retain adequate staff. Here are a few practical suggestions about how to resolve the staffing issue:

- **Adopt the motto:** "Short list of personnel and long hours of work." Most catering businesses rely mainly or entirely upon on-call staff, although larger companies employ a few permanent, full-time staff, such as a chef, kitchen manager, receptionist and sales and marketing personnel. Develop a list of reliable people to call on for work. Many people in the catering industry are willing to work long hours, so offer these people employment and the hours, before going to unknown sources.

43

- **Balance.** The key to staffing is to strike a proper balance between regular staff handling the day-to-day operations and part-timers on-call. Err on the low side when determining the size of the regular day-to-day staff; after all, it's easier to bring in additional staff, during busier times than to cut staff when it slows and ask them to come back later.

- **Payroll costs.** Normally the payroll costs, as a percentage of sales, should be between 18-30 percent. Don't forget to take into account the cost of benefits paid in addition to the hourly wages. Also, don't overtax your business with too many full-time employees. Most businesses find that payroll and benefits are their highest overhead costs.

- **Develop your fixed-cost employees.** Promote people from the variable-cost employees group. Thus, spend as much time as possible recruiting entry-level employees.

- **Personal involvement.** Bear in mind that the labor cost is your only area of flexibility. Initially, you will need to work as long as 12-14 hours a day in order to establish a positive cash flow. But, it is also likely that you'll continue to work these hours as your business grows and becomes more successful. At that point, you'll just have more company during those 12-14 hours!

- **A wise caterer knows that only happy workers are productive workers.** Remind yourself that work is not always the most important thing in Americans' lives. In fact, according to various surveys, income and standard of living is rated as only the seventh most important thing that affects the lives of Americans. That said, be sure to create proper relationships with your staff if you want to retain them.

- **Open dialog.** Give your staff feedback on their performance. When one staff member talks a great deal about what he or she did at other caterers' facilities, you have a reason to believe that he or she does the same about you. Explain to him or her how poor a policy it is to talk openly about the competition in your kitchen. Terminate that employee if this type of talk continues.

- **Be positive.** Try to present staff duties so that they don't appear to be too monotonous. During prep work, have music playing and let the prep staff control what they listen to. Keep a fun attitude with servers and make working for you a pleasant experience rather than a chore. In many people's minds, preparing and serving elegant food to classy clients is considered glamorous work. Use that in your favor when searching for catering help.

- **Do not misrepresent jobs.** In fact, it may be one of the key variables responsible for excessive employee turnover. Paint a realistic picture upfront. See to it that reality does not vary significantly from this description.

- **Multitasking.** You may hire persons with minimal or no work experience in food industry for many positions. You also need to look for employees with people skills and customer-contact skills. Many employees can work with the public and behind the scenes. But, you'll find that others greatly prefer one area rather than another. Work with people's strengths and use them to your benefit, as well as theirs.

- **Federal laws.** Be aware of federal laws that establish, for example, the minimum wage (currently $5.15 per hour). Note that you may pay people as little as $2.12 per hour, as long as the wages and their tips equal the minimum wage. At the same time take note of the Child Labor Laws that affect caterers who employ young people to bus/wash dishes and set tables. To find out more about federal labor and wage regulations, you can visit the U.S. Department of Labor at www.dol.gov.

- **INS Form I-9.** Be careful not to employ illegal aliens or tourist visitors. Complete the INS Form I-9 whenever you employ a staff worker. At the same time, take care not to engage in discrimination against any individual based on national origin or citizenship. For more information on 1-9 forms, log onto the U.S. Immigration and Naturalization Service's Web site at: www.usdoj.gov. For information about workplace discrimination, visit the Federal Consumer Information Center at www.pueblo.gsa.gov/call/workplace.html.

- **Employment tests.** Warning! Don't use employment tests to screen out people with disabilities, unless you can show that the tests are job-related and consistent with business necessity. For information concerning the American with Disabilities Act (ADA), visit the ADA home page at www.usdoj.gov/crt/ ada/adahom1.html.

Employee Recruitment

How many staff members should you hire? Before you launch into the daunting process of staff recruitment, you need to work out an overall picture for your operation. What are your staffing requirements? Recruit accordingly. Ask yourself, for instance, whether your establishment really needs a chef with prestigious qualifications, or whether a non-certified chef, head chef or working chef will fit the bill. Also, you'll probably need a kitchen manager, food preparation personnel, serving staff, on-call bartenders and a cleanup crew. Servers will often multi-task as food preparation and kitchen staff. If you specialize in wedding or banquet catering, you may need to recruit specialty serving staff such as those trained in French service, Russian service or silver service. Here are a few suggestions that will help you to recruit the right staff for your catering operation:

- **Guidelines for calculating the number of staff required versus guests served:**
    - As a rule of thumb, for a self-service hot meal, you'll need one person for every 50 guests and another person working in the kitchen.

    - For full-service meals, however, you'll need one employee in the kitchen for every 35-40 guests and one server for every 20-25 guests.

    - For tending simple bars serving wine, beer and nonalcoholic drinks, one bartender would be required for approximately 70-75 guests. For a full bar, the number of guests per bartender is reduced to 50.

    - Buffet service requires a smaller number of staff than plated events. For kitchen staff for a buffet for 50 people, you'll want one person to restock the buffet line and one in the kitchen. For service staff, you should have two to three servers and a bartender. For a plated meal, increase the kitchen staff by one and servers, by one.

- **Where will you find your potential employees?**
    - **College students.** If you live in a community with a college or university, students are good sources for on-call staff. Contact local culinary schools. They provide a good reservoir of permanent, full-time employees, as do many two-year colleges that offer hospitality management training.

- **Existing employees.** Ask them to refer people interested in working for you. Offer financial incentives for reliable referrals.

- **Homemakers and senior citizens.** Don't ignore this potential pool of staff. But, in general, avoid converting part-time senior employees into full-time ones.

- **Part-timers.** Because all caterers use part-time employees, there's a good possibility that you'll end up employing people who also work for your competitors.

- **Promote from within.** Career ladders in a company tend to attract potential employees who would not otherwise perceive your environment to be the ideal place to work.

- **Sales and management personnel.** Among the best sources are professional associations. Many catering professionals, for example, belong to the National Association of Catering Executives (NACE), www.nace.net.

- **Yipeee, Inc.** For caterers who prefer to have someone else maintain a qualified labor pool, Yipeee, Inc., www.yipeeeinc.com/home.html, of New York City, runs a database of more than 500 freelance service professionals from waiters and waitresses to maitre d's and bartenders. "We're a full-resource company that provides event management, event staffing and consulting in the catering and restaurant industry," says Karen DiPeri, Yipeee Executive Vice-President. "We screen, qualify and select seasoned service professionals. Having well-trained professionals can really make a difference at a catered event."

- **Web resources.** There are several Web sites where you can find qualified employees. Look at the National Restaurant Association's site at www.restaurant.org or the American Culinary Federation's site at www.acfchefs.org. Other sites to try include www.restaurantbeast.com and www.monster.com.

- **Screening employees.** Create a job application form that asks specific questions that are relevant to the type of personality that would fit in with your operation. Be careful when asking questions about date of birth, religion, race, marital status or number of dependents. In fact, even during an interview you should be cautious when asking the candidate about these issues. It may be simpler if you leave sensitive questions until after deciding to hire that person. However, you should definitely ask young potential staff for proof of age, if there is a minimum age requirement for the job (e.g., bartending).

- **Testing procedures.** Consider setting job applicants a simple test, such as a tray test, an integrity test, a physical exam, etc., before you qualify them for the next step in the process. A pre-employment drug test may also be included. You and other management personnel may then interview this person, especially if he or she is applying for a sales or management position.

- **An alternative screening method.** You can order a copy of Bill Marvin's "Foolproof Foodservice Selection System" at www.atlantic-pub.com. This book helps you learn how to find qualified food service staff. It also contains application forms, job descriptions, letters to applicants, tracking sheets, interview guidelines, evaluations and a variety of screening and hiring tests.

- **References.** If the candidate passes the pre-screening interview, take the time to check references. For each and every prospective member of staff? Well, the more responsible the position, the more thorough the reference-checking process should be. Always, however, check criminal records, driving records, workers' compensation records, federal and state court records, credit ratings, educational and previous employment information.

Orientation, Training and Motivation

In the busy world of catering, it's easy to skimp on this aspect of the recruitment. Do so at your peril! Time spent orienting, training and motivating new staff is time well spent. It's simple. Happy, well-informed employees are more likely to stay put and save you the hassle of going through the whole recruitment process on a regular basis. But, where do you start? Consider the following:

- **First, provide new staff with an overview.** For example, sum up your philosophy and the purpose of your business. Provide "newbies" with the employee handbook. Get the general manager to welcome them personally. Give new employees a tour of the property. Introduce them to their supervisors and colleagues. Employee handbooks for the food service industry may be found at www.atlantic-pub.com.

- **Rules.** Explain and demonstrate the main rules and regulations regarding the job on day one, not when the first problem arises.

- **Give new employees a space to call their own.** Allocate parking and locker room spaces. Also, assign them name tags.

- **Training.** Once initial orientation has been completed, start the training process. This is usually conducted in groups or consists of on-the-job training.

- **Responsibility for training.** Who does what? If your business is large enough, let the HR department carry out the general training, such as life safety, customer courtesy, complaint handling, drug and alcohol awareness, etc. Specific, job-related training is better performed by the catering department. Whatever the size of your catering operation, aim to conduct most of the training on an informal basis, interspersed with the occasional formal training program, as appropriate. High-class service, for instance, demands continual training.

- **Training guidelines.** Contact the "The Food & Beverage Committee of the Hotel Sales & Marketing Association International." It has developed training guidelines that caterers can use to make new staff familiar with all relevant operating activities.

- **Training program.** The following offer some key points to consider when setting up programs for new employees:

- **Delegate the responsibility for overseeing the training program to an established member of staff,** preferably one whose interpersonal skills you rate highly.

- **Decide how the new employees are to be evaluated, on an continuing basis.**

- **Make sure that all program content is updated regularly to reflect changes in procedures, etc.**

- **Program content.** Keep it brief. For training conducted in groups, 15-30 minutes is sufficient. Topics such as various techniques for carrying trays, creating attractive displays, cooking pasta, carving meats or serving wine properly, could be explained in one specific session. Staff involvement should be encouraged during these sessions, via discussions groups. **51**

- **Motivation.** This is the bottom line when it comes to the success or failure of any recruitment program. Learn and practice how to motivate your staff to perform to the best of their abilities and capabilities, while at the same time always keeping the clients' needs in mind. Give your employees the chance to prove themselves. Later, recognize them for their good work.

- **Foster a team spirit by:**
  - Paying your employees at least as much as your competitors and allowing for adequate employee benefits.

  - Organizing a secure working environment.

  - Providing rewards for those employees who do things right, especially from day one.

  - Disciplining those who keep doing things wrong and those who like to stir trouble.

  - Practicing firm and fair leadership.

  - Encouraging employees to solve day-to-day customer service problems themselves – and by supporting their decisions.

  - Creating opportunities for the best staff members to move up in the company.

  - Projecting a lively image by conducting upbeat staff meetings, while including staff in the planning and organization of the operation.

- **Flexibility.** Remember to remain flexible with your employees. Most catering employees work several jobs because most caterers don't hire large, full-time staffs. Your workers are going to be juggling multiple events as well as families and other responsibilities. Work with them on scheduling; if you try to be flexible with them, they will reward your efforts by being flexible and loyal!

- **National Restaurant Association's Educational Foundation.** The Educational Foundation offers many training and educational opportunities. Log onto their Web site at www.nraef.org for more information.

Compensation

It's a well-known fact that when caterers gather to discuss their trade, one of the most controversial topics is whether to pay catering staff as independent contractors or as employees. Sure, if you consider the fact that you need not pay the employer's share of Social Security and Medicare taxes, unemployment taxes or workers' compensation insurance for your independent contractors, the amount of savings could amount up to 20 percent of total payroll expenses. When considering the prickly subject of compensation, you need to be clear about the following issues:

- **Employee benefits.** What are your obligations? Required employee benefits are usually paid as payroll taxes. In addition to federal taxes, some states also require employers to contribute to their unemployment benefit programs and the state-operated workers' compensation programs. As a general rule, the minimum cost of required employee benefits equals approximately 15-18 percent of your total payroll expense.

- **Discretionary benefits.** For example, health, dental, optical and life insurance may be offered to employees at a reduced rate. Consider providing stock option plans, 401(k) plans, free meals, paid **53** vacation time and sick days, insurance coverage for dependents and formal training, etc.

- **Workers' unions.** Keep in mind that unionized properties tend to adopt generous overtime pay policies as well as very favorable holiday pay schemes. You may be required, for instance, to pay double time instead of time and a half for all overtime worked.

- **Contractors vs. employees.** Have you ever thought about the trouble you could get into with the IRS if they reclassify your independent contractors as employees? You would need to pay back the employee benefits for all those years they went unpaid, plus penalties assessed by the IRS. However, if you contract for a party and arrange for the client to pay the staff direct, then you'll need to carefully scrutinize the contract between yourself and the client. You'll also have to establish who exactly is responsible for supervising the workers – you or the client? State laws vary, so be aware of the issue. Log onto the IRS's Web site for information pertaining to federal taxes at www.irs.gov.

- **Compensation packages.** Typical compensation packages in the food service industry include salaries, wages, commissions, bonuses, tips, etc. You also need to know that:

- **Management positions usually receive predeter mined salaries.** Bonuses and commissions, however, may also be part of their compensation package.

- **Sales and marketing staff may be on monthly, weekly or hourly pay, totally on commission, or a combination of the above.** In catering, commissions usually fall in the range of 2-10 percent. But, they can vary from area to area. When calculating commission, don't forget to exclude delivery and rental charges, service charges, etc. It usually boils down to paying a commission on gross food and beverage charges. Remember, commissions reinforce productivity. Apart from your reps, also consider offering your administrative sales people who produce results, a level of ommission on top of their salaries. Don't hesitate to reward these employees.

- **Generosity.** A word of advice here: Most food preparation staffers are poorly paid, with wages slightly above minimum wage. Give your staff all that you can afford. You'll have a better chance of getting them on short notice for that last-minute event.

- **Pay for transport time.** Pay for the hours spent traveling one-way when you are transporting your staff to an off-premise catering event. It's a formula that works for both the employer and the employee.

- **Overtime**. Overtime should be pre-planned and approved by the management. It should not be confused, however, with the hours of catered events that extend beyond the planned stop time. In this situation, you'll need to pay your staff for the extra hours worked.

- **Leftovers.** When figuring the number of servings you will need for an event, plan to have enough to feed your workers. Catering and restaurant staff don't get many breaks in the real world and your staff will love you for thinking of their food needs!

Uniforms

The more formal your catering business, the more dressed up your staff should be. Having uniformed staff catering an event is more businesslike and professional. In fact, it gives the staff a sense of belonging. Make employees feel that they're members of an identifiable team. Clearly, the smartest and classiest type of outfit, for catering staff is a white tuxedo shirt, black pants and a bow tie (usually black). At the very least you should have aprons printed with your company's name and logo. Here are some general suggestions about choosing the right style of uniform for your catering operation:

Who should wear what?

- **Management.** As the owner or manager, you have the choice of wearing the same uniform as your staff. Preferably wear something at a large event that indicates you're the big boss. What do you think of a red cummerbund and a different-colored bow tie?

- **Kitchen staff.** Chefs, cooks and kitchen personnel should be in white – white shirts, coats and aprons. Hats or caps are a must.

- **Waiters/waitresses.** The traditional uniform for waitstaff is black – black pants or skirt with a white shirt and a black bow tie.

- **Part-timers.** Part-timers are generally required to maintain their own uniforms. Either have your staff buy the necessary garments, or buy a supply yourself. Give a set to each new staff member. But, be wary of deducting the cost from their paychecks.

- **Spare garments.** Have a few extra tuxedo shirts and pants available for emergencies, or a last-minute spill. Staff will appreciate your thoughtfulness.

- **General appearance and hygiene.** Insist that employees are wearing their uniforms at the start of their shift. Make it a routine that they wash their hands thoroughly before handling or serving food and that they keep their hands away from their faces and hair at all times. You are perfectly within your rights to ask staff to use an unscented deodorant and an antiseptic mouthwash, in addition to brushing their teeth frequently. A cut, scratches, bruises and injuries, no matter how minor, should be reported to the supervisor. Spitting should lead to immediate dismissal.

- **Sample Catering Dress Code:**
  - Black skirt
  - White tux shirt
  - Dark, clean, shiny shoes
  - Hair pulled back
  - No earrings for men
  - Black socks for men
  - Short and clean nails
  - Conservative makeup for women

Event Order Sheets

Make sure to provide your service staff with an event order sheet. This sheet will provide them with the information they need to make the function successful, and it will work as a list so they can double-check their equipment and food. Take a look at the following example of an order sheet:

- **Worksheet template.** You can download a template of a worksheet from www.restaurantbeast.com and see another version of a similar worksheet on www.wedoitallcatering.com.

- **Event order sheet.** Be sure to to have detailed, written instructions on every job. For an example event order sheet, see the following page.

EVENT ORDER SHEET

Customer: Judith Jones   **Contact:** Judith Jones
Phone: 555-555-5555
Event Date: 2/14/03
Event Location: J. Jones' house, 1516 Periwinkle Way
No. of Guests: 60   **Set-up time:** 5 p.m.
Event type: Coworker Christmas dinner party

SCHEDULE:

5 p.m.	caterers arrive
6 p.m.	guests arrive/serve appetizers/open bar
6:30 p.m.	serve dinner
7:45 p.m.	serve dessert
9 p.m.	guests depart

MENU:

Smoked salmon mousse on endive
Fruit and cheese display with crackers
New potatoes filled with sour cream and caviar
Beef tenderloin glazed with reduced balsamic vinegar
Wild mushroom cobbler
Roasted green beans
Bread and butter
Individual chocolate soufflé cakes

RENTALS:

Six, 60" round linens, six 10-foot rounds, two 5-ft banquet
tables for buffet.

NOTES:

Centerpieces will be delivered by florist at 5:30 p.m.
Client does not want us to use any of her personal dishes or
serving pieces.

CHAPTER FIVE

THE KITCHEN AND SERVICE EQUIPMENT

Facility Requirements and Kitchen Layout

First things first. Before you get carried away choosing equipment and accessories for your new kitchen, check out whether the location and layout meets with local zoning laws. Setting up a commercial kitchen is not always as easy as it seems! Consider the following practical issues:

- **External requirements.** Check the zoning laws and the local board of health to determine what type of permit you need to set up a commercial kitchen. Are there are any restrictions regarding hours of operation? Is the parking space adequate for deliveries from vendors or for your employees? Also, check out whether or not there are waste and septic systems in place.

- **Receiving.** Get it right. This is probably the most important area in your entire installation. In general, you'll need a counter scale of around 500-pound capacity, a portion scale for inspecting incoming products, a stand-up desk or shelf for checking packing slips and a heavy-duty hand truck for moving goods.

- **Kitchen layout.** When planning the kitchen layout, take into account the flow of food from one place to another; i.e., from receiving, through preparation, production and service, as well as supporting activities, such as dish washing, pot washing and sanitation.

- **Access.** Avoid establishing a kitchen in a building where you must use an elevator, either to enter the kitchen or to pass from one department to another.

- **Lighting.** Install adequate lighting (both gas and 220-volt electric). Maximize on natural lighting.

- **Ventilation.** Organize kitchen layout so as to make the most of natural ventilation. Also, take the extra precaution of placing ovens, ranges and steam kettles so that the mechanical exhaust units above them can operate at peak efficiency. Exhaust hoods above cooking areas should include automatic fire-fighting equipment.

- **Screens.** Place screens over all doors and windows in order to prevent fly and other insect infestation, as well as molding.

- **Garbage disposal service is essential.** The dumpster should be located near the kitchen (not close enough to attract insects).

- **Open space.** The placement of equipment should allow for sufficient aisle space. Remember, for a commissary-style operation, you'll need extra space for counting, organizing, packing, storing and shipping. For off-premises catering, it's important that you include sufficient space for all these extra activities.

- **Separate sinks.** If possible, have one sink for the chef, another one for utility work and a third for pot washing.

- **Dry storage.** The dry-storage should be dry, well-ventilated and maintained at a temperature between 55-60 degrees Fahrenheit. A thermometer should be placed in a prominent position to prevent temper-atures fluctuating outside this range. Dry-storage shelves ought to be at least 8 inches off the floor and should be convenient for "first-in, first-out" distribution. Avoid high stacking of cereal, flour and sugar. For expensive foods and equipment, a lockable valuable-items cabinet should be available.

- **Refrigerated storage.** Depending on the size of your operation, you may need one or several refrigerated storage areas. Keep in mind, however, that unnecessary large refrigerators and freezers waste energy, thus increasing operating costs. Greater refrigerated storage requirements may be justified when extra delivery charges are incurred for small quantities.

Major Equipment

You should analyze a number of factors in order to determine your equipment needs. The number of guests that you intend to serve, on a regular basis, will also help to determine the dollars you'll need to spend on equipment. Here, however, are a few basic requirements:

- **First, consider the menus you intend to serve.** For example, if you sell cold canapés, you'll need to invest in rolling racks and refrigerated storage, whereas if you sell deep-fried hors d'oeuvres, you could store the raw product in plastic containers.

- **Bar provisions.** Restrict your investment in glassware, bar utensils and beverage bars to reflect the types of services that you supply. No more, no less. If you provide alcoholic and nonalcoholic beverages, buy standard-design glasses that are easily replaceable.

- **Flatware.** Depending on the style of service, you'll need silver-plated flatware, crystal stemware, plus other first-class equipment if you specialize in upscale catering. Buy the sturdiest type plastic ware available if you cater for barbecues.

- **Don't forget about existing equipment.** This is a very important factor for off-premises caterers. For example, caterers who work frequently at party sites, where there are existing bars, won't need to bother about renting as much additional equipment for the events.

Equipment You Will Need for Your Catering Business

Your investment in kitchen equipment is something that you can usually recover if you decide to leave catering. That is because food service equipment holds its value well and re-sale is generally not a problem – provided that it's been kept in more or less good condition. That said, you'd be wise to explore the second-hand market when setting up your own business. So, where do you source your catering equipment? You'll need to acquire the following basic pieces of kitchen equipment, listed below. Take time choosing these items, as hopefully, you'll be using them day-in, day-out, for many years to come:

- **Refrigerators and freezers.** At least one separate refrigerator and one large freezer are essential. As for their size, double the minimum capacity needed for your refrigerator to keep food for a good-sized event. Don't forget that you need space for usable leftovers as well. In general, a large commercial refrigerator will accommodate all these requirements. Be aware that problems can develop; it's a good idea, therefore, to have a second freezer and refrigerator available for emergencies.

- **Ranges and hot plates.** Commercial kitchens generally favor gas stoves, which may be expensive, but they can be purchased at second-hand stores or auctions. It is quite possible to manage without a range for a long time. They take up a lot of space in your kitchen, need expensive hoods and also are costly to install. The solution? Get licensed as a "cold" kitchen. This means that you're not allowed to do frying. When the health inspector asks you about the hot plates, tell him they're for boiling water, or whatever, but never for frying! That way you can use hot plates up to a certain maximum wattage per plate and any size of convection oven, without the expensive hood!

- **Ovens.** If you don't have a range yet, start with a half-sized convection oven, which can handle three large turkeys. Convection ovens are light, portable and very convenient. But, be aware that domestic ovens and hot plates are not allowed in commercial kitchens by the board of health. Also, because they tend to dry out food, caterers are increasingly opting for the new convection steam ovens that operate as pressure-less steamers – a high-humidity convection oven.

- **Dishwashers.** Consider a commercial dishwasher with more than two racks. It saves time when storing glasses on dishwasher trays. Heat generated by dishwashers can be a problem. If so, solve the problem by installing a condenser over the dishwasher. Choose a dishwashing system that is actually engineered to meet your kitchen's requirements. Base your decision upon such factors as the space available, layout, traffic flow, amount and type of food soil and the hardness of the water.

- **Washers and dryers.** There'll be aprons, towels, napkins and uniforms to clean regularly. Invest in a robust washer and dryer from the start. Choose a large-capacity, heavy-duty model.

- **Transportation equipment.** You'll need at least one vehicle for transporting food and supplies to the party venues. Commit yourself to a professional-looking and practical vehicle. Larger operations, **63** however, will need refrigerated trucks. First, determine which truck size is the best for you (no matter what amount you anticipate carrying, your vehicle is always too small). Vans, for example, are practical and very economical for off-premises caterers that rent tables and chairs for events, instead of supplying them themselves. Trucks, on the other hand, are expensive and you may find it's more cost-effective to rent them. You may decide to have a self-contained refrigeration unit with a built-in generator, or a refrigeration unit that can be plugged into an outside power source. As for the arrangement inside, you should have a set of fixed shelves for small/medium-sized items and plenty of floor space for large equipment. Make sure that the shelves are sturdy and have a barrier of several inches around, to prevent slippage, during transportation.

- **Vehicle rental.** If you don't own a large vehicle, check into renting one. Compare rates when you call and make sure the rental company knows you are a business. If you do use rental vehicles, make sure to include the cost in your clients' estimates!

- **Holding oven.** During transportation and set-up, a holding oven, or cambro, is usually required to keep food hot. These are used to keep dinner rolls, roasts, turkeys, chicken breasts and all other hot food at the right temperature when you are transporting to the site.

- **Ice chests.** It's also a good idea to invest in some large ice chests. You will have drinks, fruit, vegetables and diary products you will want to keep cool during transportation.

- **Chafing dishes.** You'll also want to invest in two or three chafing dishes to use for buffet services.

- **Cell phones.** Cell phones are a great investment.

Sending cell phones out with your crew to event sites lets them stay in contact with you if things go wrong or if they forget something and need to send someone back. It's also a good safety measure in case the crew has vehicle trouble along the way.

- **The small stuff.** Make sure your crews always go out with the following items: dish towels, garbage bags, plastic storage bags and a first-aid kit.

Finding Equipment for Your Catering Business

- **Restaurant equipment auctions.** These provide a good source for locating catering equipment. Note, however, that these types of auctions are a bit hit and miss when it comes to finding individual smaller items. But hey, they're cheap, so buy a box of utensils just to get to get the one spatula that you're looking for!

- **Restaurant equipment stores.** For individual items and small equipment, visit second-hand restaurant equipment stores.

- **Retail shops.** You can check retail places such as Homegoods and T.J. Maxx for china and hotel-quality pans. These types of stores are often hit or miss, but if you can find what you are looking for, the price is usually right.

- **Borrow.** You should also talk to friends in the business. If they are catering part-time, you may be able to borrow equipment or split the cost and use of new equipment.

- **eBay.** This is another hit or miss source, but it's worth pursuing. Log on and register at www.ebay.com.

- **Garage sales.** Garage sales are great places to find smaller pieces of equipment such as serving platters and utensils.

- **Institution sales.** Some colleges make their old equipment available to the public at dirt-cheap prices. The items for sale can include anything from desks to fluorescent lighting to industrial fryers and steam tables. Call around to your area colleges and universities to see if such a program exists there.

Preparation Equipment

As an off-premises caterer, do you rent or purchase your preparation equipment? Well, it depends. There is a general consensus of opinion in the catering trade that, if you use a piece of equipment more than six times per year, then go ahead and buy it! Also, bear in mind the following:

- **What are the pros and cons of renting equipment?**
  - It's generally easier to pass on the costs of rental equipment than owned equipment to clients. While there is no question that the client will be charged for the equipment, with owned equipment the actual cost of ownership is not as obvious as receiving an invoice after each event.

  - You are able to obtain a much wider variety of items from rental companies.

  - On the downside, you may be dependent upon the rental company for the time of delivery of the items. Additionally, they may not deliver smaller orders, so you might have to make a larger time investment if you rent a good deal of equipment.

  - When counting equipment rented to caterers back

into their inventories, some companies miscount in their favor, while for lost/damaged equipment these rental companies bill at a replacement cost, normally higher than the actual cost.

- **Purchasing equipment.** If you decide to buy your preparation equipment, understand that it's best to buy only what is needed to meet the current business demands. Your motto should be: "Less equipment in a smaller space."

- **Small appliance "must haves."** You'd find it hard to survive without:
  - **Food processors.** While many chefs claim to be able to chop, slice or grate just as fast as a machine, it remains a fact that when you're cooking for 100 people, it's much more effective to use a machine. For smaller operations you could use a Robot Coupe food processor. However, if this type of processor is too expensive, investigate other options before buying one with all 14 plates!

  - **Mixers.** KitchenAid is the top-of-the-line mixer machine that is approved by National Sanitation Federation, www.nsf.org, for small commercial operations. If you need to mix large amounts of food, you'd be better off with a commercial machine, such as those made by Hobart, because even if you prepare dough in batches, with a domestic KitchenAid, it is extremely time-consuming. Mixers are either belt-driven or gear-driven, the latter being the more popular.

  - **Microwaves.** A microwave oven is particularly convenient for house parties where the contents of ceramic casseroles have to be reheated.

  - **Coffeemakers.** Buy at least two or three. Percolators are probably the most convenient, as you can make a large volume of coffee with minimum hassle. On the other hand, although drip coffee makers make better coffee, they require constant attention; hence they are not always very practical.

- **Electric kettles and crock-pots.** Use them to heat up water quickly for tea and for keeping food at the right temperature, either on or off the buffet table.

Kitchen and Serving Equipment

Appearances count, but so do practicalities. Take into account the image your company wants to project, but balance appearance with durability and ease of handling. For example, glass punch bowls are very difficult to pack and carry, although pretty. How about false cut-glass bowls made of plastic? Also, acidic food may react chemically with the material of certain ornate serving equipment. The following guidelines will help you choose the right types of serving equipment:

- **Price is a major consideration.** Explore the possibility of renting instead of buying. Alternatively, if purchasing, negotiate with the seller. Aim to arrive at a price between the listed price and a 50 percent reduction. Used equipment is available for significantly less money than new equipment. Consider that option when aesthetics are not your top priority.

- **A collection of knives.** Invest in the best chef's knife (sometimes called a French knife), carving knife (slicer), large serrated knife and several smaller paring knives that the budget will stretch to. Complete the collection with a knife sharpener and a sharpening stone. For special purposes, you may also need a boner and a fillet knife. Learn how to sharpen and hone your knives. Hone them regularly and sharpen them about once a year.

- **Cutting boards.** Have at least two small ones and two large ones. Look for HDP (plastic) cutting boards as opposed to wooden ones, as any odor or stain on polyethylene boards can easily be removed with a chlorine soak.

- **Scales.** Have at least three of them: one so sensitive that it can weigh a cinnamon stick accurately, one less accurate that can weigh anything from 3-10 pounds; and a third, larger scale that can weigh at least 25 pounds.

- **Pots and pans.** Acquire a collection of industrial-weight pots of all sizes. When you start, you will at least want to have a large stockpot, two large sauce pans, two small sauce pans, two large skillets and two small skillets. If you plan to offer healthy menus, you also will want to purchase pans with nonstick finishes. Some of the better brands of cookware include All Clad and Cuisinart. You'll also need several strainers. In addition, get some heavy-gauge, industrial hotel pans and sheet and half-sheet pans. They may be expensive compared with domestic pans, but you can always find them in used restaurant equipment stores.

- **Miscellaneous items.** Don't forget a substantial collection of serving equipment; e.g., platters, baskets, bowls of all shapes and sizes and serving pieces.

- **China, flatware, glassware.** It's not always easy to get this one right! If in doubt, select medium-weight dishes and dinnerware, which are both practical and attractive as well as easy to handle. Glassware also should add style and showmanship to bar offerings and to the presentation of spectacular desserts. However, keep replaceability and durability, as well as appearance, uppermost in your mind when purchasing all such items.

- **Equipment rental.** Rather than purchasing these items, consider renting them. Rental companies always have such items available. The best part about renting your china and flatware is that you simply have to rinse it off to return it! You may be able to save some labor cost by not having to wash each serving piece!

- **Logos.** If you want to have your personal logo inscribed on your china and glassware, be discreet. You mustn't appear to be advertising. Want to use them as advertising mediums? Offer individualized house drinks and special desserts in large footed hurricane glasses, or oversized parfait glasses, etched or imprinted with your business name.

- **Linens and napery.** Owning your own linen certainly has its advantages. But, it's not such a bad idea to rely on rental companies, provided that you can locate a quality supplier that doesn't cheat you with torn, mold-stained, improperly folded napkins, not to mention offerings that will be the same as other caterers using the same service. Using a rental company for linens also eliminates the need for a washer and dryer for this purpose.

- **Decorative items.** Ranging from tiny to huge ones, you can find inexpensive baskets from various sources. In addition, you'll need attractive candle holders, vases and other decorative table pieces. Start a collection of special items for specific events. Let the client think that the preparation was designed personally for them.

CHAPTER SIX

FOOD PREPARATION AND MENU

Essentials of Menu Making

Your business as a caterer is to give the customer the kind of food and service they want, when and where they want it, at the price that they specify, while still producing a profit for your company. So, the more you know about your clients, the more likely you are to meet their goals and, of course, your goals. Consider the following issues:

- **Project competence and confidence.** Use your menu as a powerful tool to project an image of a company striving to create something special, fresh and custom-designed for your client. Describe your dishes in a thoughtful manner. Avoid clichés.

- **Discuss the menu with your client.** Bring budget into the conversation at the earliest opportunity. You'll save time this way and eliminate fruitless discussions about a menu for an event that wasn't feasible in the first place.

- **Realistic goals.** Check out the capacity of the kitchen facility. This is particularly critical for off-premise catering. Check for adequate refrigeration and freezer space, size and type of ovens, stovetops, grills and any other kitchen equipment needed to prepare and hold the menu items.

Menu Trends

Keep up to date with eating and dining trends. Translate these trends to reflect your client's budget. Understand that most clients are budget-conscious – a strong demand for value is the present-day concern. However, being in fashion gives people a sense of identity. For instance, the trend towards spicier food nationwide, sparked by the Cajun craze, is now commonplace on catering menus. So don't be afraid to experiment with new menus. Keeping up with general menu trends is fairly easy. Consider the following possibilities:

- **Current trends.** There several current trends in catering you may want to be aware of when designing menus for events:

- **Stations.** For a stationed event you set up several serving areas and offer different cuisines at each. Often ethnic cuisines are used for these: one station may be Italian while the second is Chinese and a third is a dessert station.

- **Hands-on parties.** These events let people participate in the food preparation and are organized similar to a hands-on cooking class.

- **Themes.** One of the biggest trends in catering today is themes. In fact, often enough it's the food itself that determines the theme of the event. For instance, if a client wants to have Tuscan food or a South American menu, the décor and the rest of the party theme will flow from that. Because customers get tired of the same thing, themes allow you to make each event unique. Some of the most popular events could be those with a heartland cuisine or Native American foods theme. Consider turning even such basic presentations as afternoon breaks for corporate meetings into "themed" events. Or, offer a "healthy break" with granola bars and fresh fruit, for example, or a "chocoholic break."

- **Join trade organizations and subscribe to trade magazines.** This will give you access to a great deal of trend information. Three of the main trade organizations to look into are:
  - National Association of Catering Executives, 2500 Wilshire Blvd., Suite 603, Los Angeles, CA 90057, 213-487-6223

  - National Institute for Off-Premise Catering, 1341 N. Sedgwick, Chicago, IL 60610, 800-OFF-PREM

  - National Restaurant Association, 311 1st St., NW, Washington, D.C. 20001, 800-424-5156, www.restaurant.org

- **Take a look at the Restaurant Industry Forecast for 2002.** This report is available from the National Restaurant Association. The document provides information concerning forecasted restaurant industry sales and forecasted trends. Currently, industry leaders see the following trends: ethnic menus, including Mexican, Southwestern, Asian, Indian, Caribbean and Cajun; the take-out market; lean and healthy menu choices; and items made with fresh ingredients and homemade products.

- **Eat out often.** See what other restaurants and caterers are doing. What works for them and what doesn't? You can learn from your competitors' successes and mistakes!

- **Subscribe to magazines such as *Gourmet* and *Bon Appetite*.** These magazines are designed for the general public and will help you define current food and dining trends.

- **Don't forget industry magazines.** Magazines such as The American Culinary Federation's *The National Culinary Review* and *Special Events Magazine* are excellent sources for current food and dining trends as well. *The National Culinary Review* is available to members. You can find membership information on the Web at www.acfchefs.org. *Special Events Magazine* can be found at www.specialevents.com.

- **Watch television!** These days cable television is loaded with food shows with everything from the Food Network to Martha Stewart to the Iron Chef. Keeping tuned in will help you keep current!

- **Travel.** What a fun way to stay current with food trends! If you are able, travel and eat out. This will expose you to trends from other areas of the world and the country. It will also help to inspire you and spark your own creativity when working in your kitchen.

Determining What Type of Menu to Offer

Type of service partially determines type of menu. For example, the menus for a sit-down dinner for 40 and a reception for 300 are going to be very different. A menu that may work very well for a plated meal may not work at all for a buffet service event. If your customer is trying to save money, a buffet will be cheaper because of the food setup and you will not need to hire as many servers to staff a buffet as you would a plated dinner. On the other hand, if the occasion is very formal, a plated dinner would be more appropriate. Consider the following issues when trying to determine what type of menu to offer:

- **Ask your customer the following questions to determine the tone of the event.** This will help you determine the appropriate service:

- How formal is the occasion?
- How many people will be in attendance?
- Do you have any thoughts on items you would like served?
- Do you want people to mingle or to have a specific place to sit?

- **Sample menus.** Whet the client's appetite. This is your showcase. Prepare well-planned, attractive sample menus together with cost calculations. At first, work with what you know. Your confidence will grow from there. Sell the dishes that you feel most comfortable with and the ones that are your most successful. Often, the simplest are the best. Recipes can be your grandma's tried-and-true, or straight out of a magazine!

- **Steer clients away from ideas that simply won't work.** On those occasions when a client suggests an idea fraught with challenges, approach the situation carefully. Begin by complimenting them on their idea. After a moment, you slowly bring your objections to light, as though they are coming to you spontaneously, as you consider their proposal in greater depth. "That's a good idea," you might say. "I'm wondering, though; if we served such a large salad, would that make them less likely to enjoy the rest of the dinner that we're planning." (Secretly, you know that you would have to rent large salad plates for the dish the client has in mind.) "Have you seen the picture of our chef's Waldorf salad? This would make a great impression as a first course." As always, the secret to keeping everyone happy is compromise.

- **The market dictates menu needs and desires.** Never become complacent. Everyday, some other caterer will come up with a unique item and a way to present it. Most food service managers and chefs will then take that unique item and do something to make it taste even better and enhance its presentation. Play the game – improve upon others' ideas. Take the "egg," for example. It started out hard-boiled, moved up to an omelet, then became Hollandaise sauce and now it's a soufflé!

• **Special diets.** Be alert to guests with special dietary needs. Most chefs or caterers should and do accommodate special requirements. The general rule is that if it's in the building and you want it, you'll get it. The price is then adjusted accordingly and the magnitude of that adjustment depends on the magnitude of the request. Especially when planning larger events, make sure you have a vegetarian option available because the odds are you will have a vegetarian in the room. By being attuned to your customers' needs you will impress all their guests and probably find yourself getting more business from these people in the future! You should also try to have fruit to offer for dessert for anyone that may have dietary restrictions such as cardiac patients or diabetics.

Quantities and Portion Sizes

Determining portion size and quantities is tricky. Let's say you are catering a lunch party for a high school graduation. You expect 200 guests, which will include the graduates and their relatives. Your menu is grilled chicken breast served with mango salsa, pasta salad, fruit, mini focaccia sandwiches with pesto and olive tapenade and mini dessert bars. You figure each person will eat 3 ounces of chicken. As you are shutting down the buffet line, you realize you have only gone through about half the chicken! What happened? It could have been a number of things. First, at least a third of your guests were teenage girls. Teenage girls generally eat small portions, so your overage may be do to this. On the other hand, the event was held on a hot and humid afternoon, so people may have been eating lighter in general. The moral of the story is that many factors are going to affect portion size and quality; some of these you can control, others you can't. In general, however, remember: too much food is always better than too little. Here are some guidelines:

- **Some general guidelines to follow for individual portion sizes follow:**
  - Appetizers: 6 to 8 individual pieces
  - Meat entrée: 6- to 8-ounce portion for dinner; 3- to 5-ounce portion for lunch
  - Potato: 1
  - Rice: 2/3 to 1 cup
  - Pasta: 1 to 1-1/2 cups
  - Mini desserts: 2 to 3

- **Recipe guidelines.** Never plan to include a recipe in a party menu that you haven't prepared at least once before. Have the following proportions as guidelines:
  - up to 20 percent can be challenging/new recipes
  - 60-70 percent all-done-ahead-of-time recipes
  - 20-40 percent items that are purchased and that you only need to serve

Particulars of Menu Planning

Creating a winning menu is no easy task. It has to balance fantasy with reality. Above all, you want to pander to your guests, while at the same time making maximum profit – and as few costly mistakes as possible. So you'll definitely need to read on:

- **Track which items are popular (and which aren't).** Develop and use a tracking sheet to keep tabs on the popularity index of your menu items. For example, if your menu consists of items A-Z (Chicken Marsala,

House of Murphy, Lobster Thermidor, Porterhouse Steak, Veal Picatta, etc.) and, at the end of 3 months, you've sold 1,082 Marsalas, 28 House of Murphys, 486 Lobster Thermidors, 602 Porterhouse Steaks and 497 Veal Picattas, then remove House of Murphy from your menu for the next quarter, if not permanently. Offer another type of ground beef entrée in its place.

- **Balance.** Balance and timing are key factors when designing a successful, workable and profitable menu. Aim to include a range of elements from the four basic food groups: meat, fish, or other protein; fruits and vegetables; breads and cereals; plus milk and dairy products. Balance is of course about creating a meal of complementary flavors, colors, textures and harmony. For example, if you are serving a buffet dinner, you will probably have two to three entrée choices. Don't make all the choices beef; offer a beef dish as well as a seafood and vegetarian option. Keep color in mind when creating your buffet table; make sure the table isn't monochromatic!

- **Preparation time.** As you create menus, evaluate each dish for the amount of preparation time required and the cost of the ingredients. Try to strike a balance between expense and time involved. You should create a recipe file and include preparation times on your recipe cards. This will help you in determining ingredients needed and labor costs. A great resource for keeping a record of your recipes and menus and for costing is ChefTec software. You can purchase the software and find more information at www.atlantic-pub.com.

- **Timing.** Plan recipes and quantities appropriate to the time frame of the event. You may be able to serve only nibbles at a cocktail reception, for example, while if you have invited guests for a 3-hour party, the host should serve enough cocktail fare and hors d' oeuvres to provide a filling meal.

- **Service.** Important! Select the style of service that fits your party. Whether you decide on a buffet, a picnic or a formal sit-down meal, select recipes that are suited to that style. While a curried lobster bisque would be perfect for an evening wedding reception, it probably wouldn't work for the neighbors' annual summer picnic. Additionally, remember that some foods do not hold well and should not be used for a buffet.

- **Create drama.** Include intentionally dramatic elements so that you will elicit at least one "wow" from every menu.

- **Avoid repetition.** Generally, your client won't be impressed if you duplicate cooking methods or style of preparation within the same menu. Don't choose, for example, chocolate mousse for dessert, if the appetizer is salmon mousse. Also do not repeat ingredients on the menu.

- **Rotate your menus.** Take market conditions into account. Develop new menus seasonally. Have alternative plans up your sleeve should a product become unavailable or priced out of your budget. In fact, it's standard in the food service industry for quality food service establishments to change their menus every quarter. The rule of thumb is to track your mix. Replace less-popular items with new ideas, every 3 months.

Food Preparation

Time is a critical element when you're a caterer and timing even more so. Many foods can be prepared several days, even weeks or months, in advance and wrapped and stored in either your refrigerator or freezer. Here are a few suggestions to help you streamline your food-preparation procedures:

- **Advance preparation.** Prepare the following dishes the day before:
  - Cheese trays (covered and refrigerated, minus the crackers)
  - Fruit and vegetables (except strawberries), cut and bagged
  - Pastries (bake)
  - Fruit and vegetable trays (arranged)
  - Dips
  - Pastries (stuffed)
  - Meats that require sauces (in most cases)
  - Vegetables
  - Cheese blocks
  - Breads and crackers

- **Vegetables.** On the day of an event, store broccoli, carrots, celery, cauliflower and radishes in an ice bath to keep them fresh and crisp. A vegetable tray for a typical event might contain chopped broccoli, celery, carrots, cauliflower, cucumbers, yellow squash, zucchini and radishes. If you're serving 100 guests, you'll need about 10 pounds of vegetables (net weight).

- **Fruit.** For the fruit trays, peel, core, remove seeds and chop/slice honeydew, cantaloupe, strawberries, blueberries, raspberries, bananas, oranges and apples. A fruit tray for 100 guests will require around 20 pounds of fruit (net weight). Some fruits, such as apples and bananas, have to be kept in lemon juice to prevent them from turning brown. Don't wash strawberries until the last minute; they get soggy quickly!

- **Sandwiches.** Many events offer small sandwiches for guests. Slice any meats, such as roast beef, ham, turkey or salami, on the day of an event, to prevent them from drying out. This also applies to the accompanying vegetables and garnishes such as lettuce, tomato and red onion. Sliced cheese should be laid out and presented attractively. If you're serving 100 guests, you'll need approximately 20 pounds of meat for sandwiches on cocktail breads. For regular-sized sandwiches, you'll need about 30 pounds of meat per 100 guests.

- **Breads.** Place a moist paper towel on top of the breads/rolls until just prior to service to keep them soft and moist. (Remember, most breads become hard and unpalatable if left out even for a few minutes.) Use miniature seeded rolls for an added touch. They seem to hold up longer (stay soft) as opposed to the typical cocktail breads (that dry out quickly). Also offer cocktail rye, wheat and pumper-nickel.

- **Seafood.** Seafood items need careful attention. No shortcuts here! Fresh fish, including salmon and trout, must have clear, glassy eyes (not cloudy) and must be slime-free. Avoid seafood or fish that smells of ammonia – a clear indication that it's unfit for consumption!

- **Punch.** When using a punch fountain, don't use a punch recipe that has sherbet or any kind of fruit pulp – the particles will clog up the fountain. Serve this type of punch recipe from a glass or crystal punch bowl instead.

- **Other preparations.** Plan ahead. A full-service caterer may spend the week before an event preparing food, decorating the event space, underlining plates with doilies, polishing silver and mirrors and folding napkins – anything, in fact, that can be handled ahead of time. Attend to little details. Clean and polish utensils such as tongs, spoons and ladles.

- **Get the customer involved.** This approach to food "preparation" is becoming an increasingly popular trend. Today's sophisticated guests like to participate and show off their culinary skills. Consider setting up an action (or assembly) station. Introduce hands-on customer involvement for some aspects of the food preparation. How about a "tartar station" where guests are invited to select their salmon, beef or other raw meats? Let them put the meat through the appropriately labeled grinder themselves and position their plates to catch it. Definitely a very bonding, team-building "session" that works as both entertainment and meal service.

Catering for Beverage Functions

Beverage functions can be held for a variety of reasons. In order to plan effectively for a "drinks do," the caterer needs to discuss priorities with the client beforehand. For instance, is the main purpose purely social where guests can recharge their batteries, or is it designed to offer an opportunity for networking? Whether a beverage function is scheduled to take place before or after a meal will also affect the types of drinks to be served at that function. Clarify all these issues with your client. This way you'll be able to suggest the type of event that exactly meets their requirements. Bear in mind the following:

- **Knowledge.** Off-premises caterers, in particular, must be knowledgeable about the brands and qualities of various beverages. Clients are guaranteed to ask for your advice. Expertise in this area may mean the difference between being selected or rejected by the client.

• **Be wary if your client insists on providing the bartenders.** They may not be adequately trained or capable of performing to your high standards. Smoking behind the bar is a common complaint. Guests would assume that the bartenders are part of your staff. This would inevitably reflect poorly upon your services and damage your reputation through no fault of your own.

• **Formal/traditional beverage functions.** Stick to the tried and tested. For this type of function, most clients prefer a standard drinks' menu: red and white wine, a domestic light and regular beer, some soft drink brands, drink mixtures and at least one brand of each Scotch, gin, vodka, bourbon, rum, tequila and Canadian whiskey.

• **Informal functions.** Develop a fashionable drinks' menu. Cater for today's preferences for reduced alcohol or alcohol-free beverages. Current trends indicate a decline in the sale of alcoholic beverages, particularly hard liquor, with a corresponding increase in the sales of light, imported and microbrew beers, as well as specialty drinks. Make sure, however, that you retain vodka on the drinks' menu; statistics confirm that it is still the most popular spirit amongst females. The same applies to Scotch for males.

• **Cater to suit your guests' preferences.** Tastes vary depending on location and audience. Be aware of the fact that there are geographic differences in the consumption of spirits. For instance, the number of drinks consumed on average, per person, at a black-tie gala with reception and dinner in Las Vegas is 5.5, in Chicago it's 5.0, and in San Francisco, it's only 2.5 drinks per person. **83**

- **To calculate required beverage quantities, use the following formula:**

  Total ounces = number of guests x average number of drinks per person x ounces per drink

- **To work out the total quantity, divide the total ounces by the bottle size.**

- **For soda and juices, take the total number of bottles of spirits and multiply by 3.** And the ice: 2-3 pounds per person.

- **Pricing.** Bear in mind that most clients are more concerned about the price per drink, price per bottle, labor charges, etc., than about specifying the brand names to be served at the catered event. Consider using a simple pricing procedure where guests pay, personally, for each drink. The most common pricing procedure for open bars is to charge per bottle. For combination bars, the host may decide to pay for each guest's first drink. The guests then pay for any subsequent drinks. Another option is "a limited-consumption bar," where the host establishes a dollar amount that he is prepared to spend. When the cash register reaches that amount, the bar is closed, or reopened as a cash bar.

- **Wine.** During a normal reception period, the overall consumption of wine averages three glasses per person. Offer a choice of wines assuming a ratio of 4 white: 1 red, since so many people prefer white wines. When pricing wines, don't forget to put a higher markup on low-cost items and a lower markup on high-cost items. For instance, a wine that costs $5 per bottle wholesale will be acceptable if priced at $15, whereas a wine that costs $10 will be more acceptable if priced at $20.

- **Beer.** Include beer on your drinks menu. Beer is no longer considered "low-class," and women are increasingly drinking this beverage.

- **Minimize wastage.** Don't open all the bottles of wine ahead of time. Open the designated wines just before or just after the appropriate dish of a meal is served.

Legal Implications of Alcoholic Beverage Catering

The beverage caterer needs to be fully aware of state and local municipality liquor laws, as well as the legal implications of providing bartenders to serve alcoholic beverages. The following information will help you navigate the complex business of catering for an alcoholic beverage function:

- **To sell alcoholic beverages, you must have a license to sell.** For off-premise caterers, there are three possible scenarios:

  - **You may be permitted to serve, but not sell** alcoholic beverages. In this case, you have to provide payment to the retail liquor vendor, with the client's check payable to that liquor vendor, for the amount of purchase.

  - **You may obtain a temporary license** to sell liquor at a specific event, at a specific date and time.

  - **In some states (e.g., California),** you can obtain a license to sell and serve alcohol on a regular basis. For example, a restaurant operator who is licensed to sell alcoholic beverages at the restaurant, may apply for a license to sell at off-premises events.

- **An on-premises caterer must have the right type of license to serve liquor.** A full tavern license is usually needed to serve spirits, wines and beers. Be aware, also, that in some parts of the country, a hotel or conference center may not be able to serve liquor if it does not possess a private club license.

- **Serving alcoholic beverages to minors is a serious offense.** You cannot sell alcoholic beverages to anyone under 21 years old, except (in some states) in the presence of his or her parents or legal-age spouse.

- **Do not serve alcoholic beverages to intoxicated individuals.** While there is a legal criterion for considering a person to be intoxicated (a blood alcohol concentration of .08-.10, depending on the state), there is no sure-fire way of telling whether a person is intoxicated or not. Play safe – don't serve alcohol to anyone who appears to be intoxicated.

- **"Cut off" that person by trying to minimize the confrontation.**

- **The consequences of serving an intoxicated guest.** Beware, if you serve an intoxicated guest or a minor and he or she goes out and causes an accident, the facility, server and host may be liable for damages to the injured person. In some states, under dram shop legislation, you'll be held at least partially responsible – you cannot defend yourself if it is proved that the facility's employees served a minor or a legally intoxicated guest.

- **Social-host laws.** Some states have social-host laws; other states have neither dram shop nor social-host laws. But whichever way you look at it, you don't want to get involved in a legal battle that could ruin your business.

- **Beverage functions that do not offer food.** Check with the Alcohol Beverage Commission. Establish whether you're allowed to cater for an alcoholic beverage-only function. The Alcohol Beverage Commission will also be able to advise you of the rules regarding clients who want to bring in their own liquor. You may, for instance, be prohibited from offering free liquor or reduced-price liquor.

- **Alcoholic portion regulations.** To avoid overcompensation of alcohol, some local municipalities restrict the amount of alcohol you can put into each drink. You may not be allowed, for example, to serve doubles, boilermakers and pitchers of beers, or traditional Mudslides, Long Island Iced Teas and Scorpions (the last three because they contain multiple liquors).

Preventing food-borne illnesses is essential to the success of your catering operation.

CHAPTER SEVEN

SANITATION, HEALTH & SAFETY PROCEDURES

Causes of Food-Borne Illnesses

Food safety is of critical importance. A food-borne illness outbreak could ruin your business and have severe legal ramifications. Worse, when it does occur in the catering trade, it rarely affects one person alone. Most of the time, sickness spreads rapidly to affect the majority of guests and you end up with your catering operation emblazoned across the front page of the local newspaper! Guests are quick to compare notes and to conclude that they've all eaten or drank the same things. The odds of you being sued are high, not to mention that your reputation will be ruined, overnight. Needless to say, preventing food-borne illnesses is essential to the success of your business. Consider the following important issues:

- **Avoid physical, chemical and biological contamination.** Keep hair tied back and covered during food preparation. Avoid using metal equipment with flaking surfaces. Take special care to avoid chemical contamination caused by substances such as cleaning compounds, additives or pesticides. Bacteria, however, are one of the main causes of food-borne illnesses. Be particularly vigilant when preparing foods, such as eggs, meat, poultry, fish, milk products, etc. These food items are a dangerous breeding ground for bacteria.

- **Viruses.** Viruses are other biological items that cause food poisoning. Make sure that food handlers wash their hands between the preparations of each food item. It's the simplest and best way to prevent the spread of viruses by food handlers. Also, have it written into employees' contracts that they wash their hands thoroughly after using the restroom, sneezing, coughing or touching their mouths with their hands. This is not overkill. Your livelihood is at stake.

- **Ignorance can be lethal!** Grasp the basics about the following:
  - **Salmonella.** Found in poultry and meat, raw eggs (used in mayonnaise), as well as prepared foods such as chicken and ham salads. Salmonellosis can be caused by poor personal hygiene of the food workers using unsanitized utensils.

  - **Staphylococcus aureus.** A very common bug, creating toxins in foods; e.g., ham products, salads, milk products and cream-filled desserts. Be particularly careful with foods that require a lot of handling because the Staph bug is easily transmitted amongst staff. If food is left at a dangerous temperature for too long, you can no longer rely on heat or cold to destroy the bug. Make sure that foods are maintained at a temperature below 45° F or above 140° F. Never store food at room temperature. The risks are too great. Note that Staphylococcus aureus can be carried by healthy people. It thrives in cuts, burns and other infections. It is spread by sneezing, coughing or touching the skin. Employees with infected cuts, burns or boils should be excluded from food handling and ware-washing.

  - **E. Coli.** Found in the intestines of cattle, contamination usually takes place in the slaughterhouse. E. Coli is found in ground beef, roast beef, hamburgers and unpasteurized milk. To kill this bacterium, cook beef at a minimum temperature of 155° F.

- **Shigella, Campylobacter jejuni, Listeria, Yersinia.** Poor personal hygiene and sloppy food handling are the causes of food contamination by these bacteria. Campylobacter is frequently found in poultry and unpasteurized milk. Listeria thrives in soft cheese and paté left in warm, moist conditions, in insufficiently cooked chicken, as well as in unhygienically prepared salads.

- **Clostridium botulinum and Clostridium perfringens.** Clostridium botulinum causes botulism and is found in canned foods. Avoid serving foods from cans with severe dents or bulging tops. Clostridium perfringens, on the other hand, is found predominantly in meat and poultry. Contamination occurs when these items are not properly cooked, cooled or reheated.

- **MSG.** Beware the risks associated with another form of food poisoning – the so-called reaction to Monosodium Glutamate. Many Chinese restaurants rely heavily upon its flavor-enhancing qualities. MSG actually changes the flavor of foods.

- **Here are a few Web sites that can provide you with more information on food-borne illnesses and allergies:**
  - Center for Disease Control, www.cdc.gov
  - National Restaurant Association's Educational Foundation, www.nraef.org
  - International Food Information Council, www.ific.org

Employee Hygiene

Personal hygiene is a delicate issue, at the best of times. But, in the catering trade, you have no option but to tackle the matter head-on. It may seem awkward to address the people who work for you, on the subject of personal cleanliness, but you really have no choice. Here are some guidelines:

- **State your employee hygiene rules in writing.** The easiest way to deal with issues of employee hygiene is to produce a written list of rules and regulations. Give a copy to all members of staff. Here are some suggestions to help you get your message across:

  - If an employee appears ill, or even has a cold, he or she should not handle food.

  - Employees must routinely wash their hands before starting work and after visiting the restroom.

  - Hand washing should be done with hot water and soap for at least 20 seconds. (Sad to say, it is the most common source of food contamination.)

  - Kitchen employees should use disposable plastic gloves when handling food. Gloves should never be worn, however, when working around heat sources.

  - Hats or hairnets should be worn in all food preparation places.

  - Jewelry should not be worn when working in the back-of-the-house, while front-of-the-house staff may wear minimal jewelry.

  - Staff should never touch the eating end of flatware, or the rims of glasses, bowls, plates and cups.

- Dropped flatware, napkins and tableware items should be replaced with clean items.

- **Staff should be knowledgeable about food allergies.** Employees should be certain when guests ask if a particular food contains a certain ingredient. To find out about food allergies, contact the International Food Information Council at 202-296-6540, or visit their Web site at www.ific.org.

- **Sanitation regulations.** Be sure to post sanitation standards and policies in a prominent position in all food production and ware-washing areas.

Sanitation Inspections

Local and state boards of health make frequent and unannounced inspections at all food establishments. You cannot afford to let standards slip, even momentarily. Bear in mind the following:

- **The Educational Foundation of the National Restaurant Association.** The National Restaurant Association is the foremost training and testing leader for foodservice sanitation throughout the USA. Consult www.atlantic-pub.com for information on the ServSafe™ course. This course provides foodservice managers with basic sanitation principles, as well as methods for training and motivating employees to follow sound sanitation practices.

- **Culinary programs.** Check your area colleges and vocational schools for culinary programs as well. These programs usually offer a course in food safety and sanitation. Upon passing the course, the individual will be certified in food safety and sanitation by the state.

- **Legislation.** Note that in many states, some form of sanitation certification is mandatory.

- **Foods must come from approved sources** and be wholesome and unadulterated (legal and USDA-inspected). For more information on the USDA, visit www.usda.gov.

- **Meat must be inspected by the USDA** and carry a stamp of approval on the meat carcass, or a tag on poultry.

- **Fish and frozen foods must be certified by the U.S. Public Health Service (www.hhs.gov/phs).** Fishing sources and fish processing must be certified by the U.S. Department of the Interior.

- **Milk, eggs, fruits and vegetables should be inspected by the USDA.**

- **Food must be protected against all potentially hazardous agents** and maintained in temperature-controlled areas during the storage, preparation, service and transport.

- **Personnel must wear clean clothes,** effective hair restraints and practice good personal hygiene.

- **Utensils and equipment must be kept clean;** pots must be free of grease and carbon accumulation.

- **With respect to garbage and rubbish storage and disposal,** a number of covered, rodent-proof, clean containers should be available.

- **Floors, walls and ceilings must be properly constructed,** in good repair and drains must be in working order. Mats must be removable, clean and in good repair. Lighting must be adequate and fixtures must be clean. All rooms and equipment hoods must have ducts vented as required.

- **Clean and soiled laundry** must be properly stored.

Food Handling

The job of everyone in the catering industry is to avoid contamination of food during storage, preparation and service. Bacteria growth in food occurs when food temperatures are in the danger zone of between 45-140° F. It is vital that everyone on your staff understands that foods must be brought through this zone from cold to hot and hot to cold as quickly as possible. Anyone handling food should be fully aware of the following:

- **Room temperature.** Avoid leaving any food that needs refrigeration at room temperature for more than an hour, a maximum of two, before serving.

- **Ideal food temperatures.** Use a probe thermometer to ensure that foods are maintained at the following temperatures:

- **Frozen food and freezer temperatures should be between 0-15° F** (for frozen poultry, meat, fish, frozen fruits and vegetables and ice cream).

- **Cold food at below 40° F.**

- **The refrigerator temperature must keep food between 32-40° F.**

- **Hot food at a minimum of 165° F.**

- **Reheated foods should reach a minimum of 165° F and be kept at that temperature until served.**

- **Milk.** Use only pasteurized milk and milk products that are kept below 45° F.

- **Ice cream.** Serve ice cream with a scoop located in a dipper well with running water, in a clean and dry container, or in the actual ice cream container.

- **Avoid using recipes that contain raw eggs.** Better safe than sorry. Raw eggs, for example, should not be used in Caesar salad or other dishes that require little or no cooking.

- **Mayonnaise.** Handle mayonnaise with extreme caution. It's often the cause of food poisoning, particularly when it's left out in the sun or a warm location. If mayonnaise isn't kept at the correct temperature, it will rapidly start to separate into its various ingredients and breed offensive bacteria. Also, if exposed to open air, mayonnaise acts as a magnet for insects that deposit eggs or germs.

- **Outdoor catering.** Keep all food that requires refrigeration under wraps and at an ambient temperature until the last minute. Try to find a shady spot for setting up the food displays.

- **"When in doubt, throw it out!"** Discard any food that has been exposed to warmth for too long. It just isn't worth risking your reputation, or the health of your guests, for that matter.

- **Transportation.** Pre-chill foods that are to be served cold before you transport them to the venue. Keep these foods at a temperature of 45° F for both storage and service. Keep foods that are to be served hot, at a temperature of 165° F or above. For off-premise caterers, it is very important to understand that during food transportation, the risk of contamination is great. Carry all food, serving equipment and utensils in securely wrapped packages. Whether chilled or cooked, foods should be maintained in constant, controlled temperatures, at all times.

Safety Procedures

Safety is a top priority issue. Don't leave anything to chance. Rules regarding safety procedures should be well-documented and posted in a prominent position. Also, all employees must be 100-percent familiar with official procedures in the event of an emergency. Reassess and update ways in which you can reduce the risks of accident for both employees and clients alike. Make sure that the following safety measures are implemented (and adhered to) at all times:

- **Floors.** Keep floors clean, dry and in good repair. Use signs such as "Caution" and "Wet Floor" as appropriate.

- **Only allow trained staff to operate specific equipment.** Protective goggles and gloves should be worn while operating hazardous machinery. Also, only use equipment for its designated purpose.

- **Keep your knives sharp.** Blunt knives are a common cause of both minor and major injuries. When using a knife, cut foods with fingers curled under. Cut away from the body, and make sure all your kitchen employees know the proper way to handle knives.

- **Train your employees in correct lifting and transporting methods.** Teach your employees the correct procedures for carrying heavy items and trays.

- **Keep beverages away from fryer stations.** Cold beverages spilled into the hot fryer can cause major eruption of hot grease.

- **Ovens.** All ovens, broilers and grills fueled by large tanks of propane should not be used indoors. Also, you may need a special permit from local authorities to use butane fuel indoors.

- **Fire.** The ultimate dread of any caterer! Locate fire extinguishers strategically throughout the establishment. Make sure that an extinguisher is available near each potential fire source. Also, keep at least one fire extinguisher in each catering vehicle.

- **First-aid kits should be located on your premises and in your transportation vehicles.** Teach your employees the Heimlich Maneuver. Remember, choking can happen at any time, but particularly when a person who has had a bit too much to drink or gobbles their food too quickly.

- **Accident log.** Complete an accident report for all accidents, however major or minor. Forward a copy to the caterer's workers' compensation insurer, the Occupational Safety and Health Administration (www.osha.gov) and the insurance company providing business insurance.

- **Emergency first-aid procedures.** If someone collapses, for whatever reason, the single most important thing is to ensure that they can breathe properly. Remove belts, bras and corsetry immediately, if they constrain circulation or breathing. Also, watch out for the danger of swallowing false teeth or tongues. Don't neglect victims of alcohol. They can easily "drown" by choking on their own vomit after becoming unconscious.

CHAPTER EIGHT

FOOD PRESENTATION

Creating the "Wow!" Factor

Today's clients expect more than quality food at a catered event; they want their socks knocked off by the food presentation as well. "People do eat first with their eyes," says Frank Puleo, owner of Framboise Catering in New York City, vice president of Culinary Expressions International and NCA president. When it comes to presentation, take a tip from Puleo, who often caters at exotic venues. For example, Puleo catered one recent event at the Air France terminal in the Newark, New Jersey, airport. "The husband was taking his wife to Paris for her 40th birthday and wanted a surprise party with a few of their friends and family as a send-off," says Puleo. To dazzle guests, Puleo employed an in-house artist to customize each catered event from passing platters to plate presentations. For a recent event at the Rock and Roll Hall of Fame Museum, the artist arranged the food around 45s and small guitars on the serving and passing trays. "We use a lot of different vegetables to try to get a mix of color, texture and height on a plate and garnish with fresh herbs," says Puleo. Here are some suggestions for wowing guests with your presentation:

- **"People eat with their eyes first, not their mouths."** Make food attractive so you can turn even the simplest foods into something wonderfully appealing! Presentation must be visually appealing. To be a successful caterer, food must be good, but so should the food presentation. It takes creativity, common sense and pride to achieve the perfect results. If you have a crudités display, for example, try cutting the vegetables into interesting designs: make radish roses and carrot flowers. Make sure you garnish plates and platters and do not overload the plates with food.

- **"T" or serpentine arrangement.** Use this proven-successful setup for wedding receptions. A "T" arrangement allows guests to serve themselves from both sides of the table, thus preventing long lines and allowing more time for socializing. Display the food in a "lust" setting.

- **Personalize the layout for each event.** For example, decorate the tables with flowers of every color, or shining silk and lamé fabric. Alternatively, use glass block and mirrors. You also can create height on the buffet table by putting boxes or cake stands under the tablecloths and putting some platters on top of these stands. Think about the personality of the client as well. Does the bride have a fondness for a particular flower? Incorporate these into the centerpieces.

- **The elegant dessert.** For guaranteed "wow," serve a stunning dessert such as "The Three Berries" dessert. It consists of a dish of fresh berries arranged on leaves, then a simple sauce of creme fraiche, or raspberries, served separately. There is nothing complex about this dessert – it's the presentation that it makes it special. Keep it simple, but go for impact. If you are not comfortable with your baking skills (as many caterers are not), find an excellent bakery to make your desserts. To find a dessert supply, check with area restaurants. Most restaurants do not have in-house pastry chefs anymore, so if you find one that has wonderful desserts, ask the owner or manager who supplies them.

- **"Less is more."** Create an exquisite carrot "chrysan-themum" Simply place a tiny sorrel and scallop soufflé on a nest of beet purée. It's sure to impress your guests and is far more effective than a platter decorated with a mass of fluted vegetables and piped decorations. The key to achieving impact is to arrange foods with a sense of scale and proportion.

- **Create an illusion of effortlessness.** One of the best secrets of effective food presentation is to make it look as if it's been effortlessly prepared. Achieve this effect by placing your food in interesting patterns. Choose an exquisite garnish, or decorate the platter with a single ingredient. This strategy never fails.

- **Tailor your arrangements to reflect a client's individual requirements.** Pay special attention to the different dishes being presented, as well as their size. Put dynamic patterns into use. Nothing can be more boring than seeing all dishes on a table arranged statically in the same manner!

Guidelines for Tray and Platter Selection and Design

Choose service platters according to the occasion. Consider the color of food when deciding on which serving dishes to use. In general, vivid dishes stand out against white backgrounds, while, at the same time, showing off your food to its best advantage. Aim to achieve the following:

- **Focal point.** Introduce a focal point – an area on the platter or dish to which the eye is automatically drawn. For instance, the platter setup might consist of straight and curved lines, with a centerpiece of salad garnish cascading from the focal point. Perhaps, try to create a straight-line effect, with lines radiating from the centerpiece.

- **"Construction."** When preparing a tray or platter, make sure that the food is properly molded, cooked, sliced, faced or sequenced.

- **Height.** This is another important factor of presentation. Create an illusion of height by positioning a large piece of unsliced roast or galantine in the center of the platter; a rack of ribs is always an impressive option. Or, build a stack of sliced meats with whole pieces of fruit interspersed between the layers. Consider, also, using an acorn squash filled with a sauce or salad. Do not over stack or over-portion a plate.

- **Think of the plate as a canvas and see what you can create.** As an example for a plated dinner, rather than just putting the sliced roast pork beside the mashed potatoes and the green beans, tie the pieces together. Place the mound of potatoes in the center of the plate and fan the slices of pork around it leaning against the mound. Tie the green beans into a bundle with a steamed chive and angle them on the other side of the potatoes.

- **Balance.** Achieve balance, either symmetrically or asymmetrically. In general, food items gain visual weight by their color, size and texture. Layout must be cohesive as well. Arrange the components on a plate in such a way as to appear as a single offering that works well together. In other words, unify the dish so that there is also no competition between items. Keep it simple.

- **Line.** Line is important because a strong line has strong eye appeal. A strong line helps to draw the guest's eye to the plate.

- **Color.** Don't forget to think about color and texture in plate presentation. Try to get maximum eye appeal. Perhaps top your salmon with some red pepper curls or chopped chives.

- **Eat-ability.** Finally, keep in mind that the guest is eventually going to eat the masterpiece you have just created. Don't make it difficult to reach around garnishes or to cut into food.

- **Display unattractive dishes in exciting or special tableware.** Dishes such as creamed chicken, chili, etc., will immediately appear more enticing.

Essentials of Presentation, Garnishing and Arranging

The first rule for making your guests "wow" at your food is, of course, to make it taste good. But that's not what food preparation is all about! There's much more to presentation. So, while taste is affected by proper seasoning, execution of basic cooking principles, consistency and quality of product, appearance is the other important factor that you cannot ignore. In general, the factors that affect presentation are proper food arrangement, composition, appropriateness and uniformity when cutting vegetables, meats, etc. Also, bear in mind the following considerations regarding food presentation:

- **Diagrams.** Create diagrams in order to organize your thoughts for food presentation. This will help you in placing, sizing and shaping your foods. It is time well spent.

- **Simplicity.** Strive to create a very simple visual statement. In other words aim for light, elegant touches instead of massive, complex constructions.

- **Try to balance taste, color and texture.** Let your style of garnishing and decorating become your personal statement. Try to reflect your dedication to and enthusiasm for catering. It may be the use of a lemon slice, the way you twist edible garnishes or a corn fritter – it doesn't matter as long as you get your point across.

- **For maximum impact, introduce a wide variety of textures.** Foods need to be crunchy, silky, chewy, velvety – any distinct texture. At the same time, offer intense flavor; for instance, wrap foods (and not just a tortilla around grilled chicken and beans). Take "Cannelloni alla Sorpresa" – Mamma Mia! The "surprise"? Well, the cannelloni is filled with tortellini. Alternatively, include in your menu salmon wrapped inside a lettuce leaf and a macadamia crust on sea bass.

- **Blend colors and textures.** Harmonize colors and textures and get the guests ooh-ah-ing. Voilà! Success on a plate! Achieve this by avoiding non-functional garnishes, edible or inedible, that don't contribute to the taste or texture of the dish. For example, leaves of lettuce used as under-liners for hors d'oeuvres on hot plates, tomato roses and apple birds, or a crown of lemon on a dish that has a sauce served with it, are unnecessary garnishes that should be avoided.

- **Contrast.** Achieve contrast in color and texture by serving two vegetables, one green and one other color – simple, but effective. Maybe add a drizzle of vegetable custard? Or, garnish the roasted green beans with red peppers curls.

- **Highlight color.** Highlight the overall color of a dish with a second color. Create excitement. For example, yellow dishes such as saffron rice and rutabaga look nicer with red or green accents. Perhaps use intense shades of color that make the food stand out.

- **New ideas.** Always be on the lookout for fresh ideas. Take a look at various magazines and cookbooks. Develop your very own sense of garnishes and decorations. Never become jaded – be prepared to experiment.

Make a Splash!

The following suggestions offer tried-and-tested ways of really making a splash! Consider incorporating some of them into your repertoire:

- **Create a Napoleon appetizer.** Layer crisp phyllo pastry or deep-fried wonton layers with savory fillings.

- **Try a fresh look for the classic Mexican seven-layer dip.** Instead of serving this in the traditional-style dish, try serving it in individual portions in a martini glass.

- **A fish cooked whole.** Leave the head on. Deep fry, roast or steam the fish.

- **Butterfly (spatchcock) a chicken or other fowl.** Grill it flat.

- **Use a mandolin.** Slice Yukon gold potatoes, fry them and use these for salad croutons.

- **Wild rice waffle.** Use it as the base for a savory appetizer.

- **Sweet tamales of walnut and cinnamon.** Serve with crema fresca.

- **Add a twist to serving caviar.** Combine with a vodka tasting session.

- **An entrée with impact.** Serve a 10-inch porcini mushroom with minimal garnish.

- **Salmon.** Cut it into strips and interlace the strips to create a basket weave square for steaming.

- **Jumbo Thai prawns.** Grill in the shell. Serve on a giant banana leaf.

- **Blackberry and blueberry sorbets.** Serve in hot-pink tulip glasses.

- **Peaches (with the stem on).** Poach in red wine with cardamom-vanilla sauce.

- **Heart-shaped ravioli.** Serve on a brilliant red sauce for a Valentine appetizer.

- **Edible flowers and flower petals.** Add these to salads and desserts for that extra-special touch.

- **Here are some extra tips on how to make a presentational splash:**
  - Instead of sifting confectioners' sugar, cocoa, cinnamon or ground nuts through commercial paper doilies, let your imagination soar by making your own templates. Trace designs on manila file folders, then cut out using a razor-sharp box cutter or mat knife.

  - To make red or yellow pepper curls, fillet the peppers and slice in very thin strips. Put the strips in ice water for several hours and they will curl.

  - Fry sage leaves to top poultry or pork dishes.

  - For a festive touch, dust mint sprigs lightly with confectioners' sugar before using to garnish a dessert plate or platter.

  - To "paint" the sauce on a dessert plate, pool a little of the sauce in the bottom of a plate. Then, with a second sauce of contrasting color in a squirt bottle with a fine tip, make a series of concentric circles in the first sauce. Finally, at regular intervals, draw a knife tip or poultry pin across the sauce rings, creating a spider web effect.

- To "paint" hearts in sauce, squirt the second sauce into a ring of dots, spacing them about an inch apart. Stick a knife tip or poultry pin in the center of a dot, pull it to the right or left, up or down, forming a heart. For two-toned hearts, place a smaller dot of contrasting color inside each large dot.

- To save time, pipe rosettes or dollops of whipped cream on to foil-covered baking sheets and freeze. Transfer to self-sealing plastic bags, label and date and store in the freezer. Then all you need to do to dress up a dessert is top each portion with a rosette or dollop of frozen whipped cream. They will thaw in 10 minutes or less.

- **The menu.** Don't underestimate the power of the written word. How you describe your dishes, on the menu, is an important aspect of food presentation. For instance, instead of simply listing "hors d'oeuvres," menus could refer to the items as a variety of hot and cold hors d'oeuvres presented on silver platters by tuxedoed waiters. Likewise, menus shouldn't allude just to a "buffet," but rather, to a "a sixteen-foot, textured-fabric-draped buffet with our staff serving each of your guests." And, of course, menu prices should never be presented as "per person," but as the more inviting "per guest."

*Continual marketing is
vital to your success.*

CHAPTER NINE

MARKETING & PRICING

Why Marketing is Mandatory

Marketing is mandatory, not only when setting up your catering business, but also on a continuing basis. In fact, it's absolutely essential in order to ensure the long-term success of your enterprise. Your goal as a smart caterer is to find new markets for your products and services. But first of all, you'll need to think carefully about which market you want to target. Select the advertising medium that is best able to reach your target audience. Try the following approach to marketing:

- **Define your market.** The first step in any marketing program is to undertake a full and detailed analysis of your potential clients in the local marketplace. First, decide what kinds of clients appeal to you. Do you want to cater small, intimate parties or large-scale events? Once you have defined the type of catering operation you want to own, you can start analyzing your potential customers. To define your niche, you need to know your area's demographics. You can find a great deal of demographic information on the U.S. Census Bureau's Web site at www.census.gov. Additional Web sites that can provide demographic information are listed below.

- **American Fact Finder.** This Web site, located at factfinder.census.gov/servlet/BasicFactsServle, lets you search, browse and map U.S. Census data, including economic, population, geographical and housing statistics.

- **CACI Information Decision Systems.** This site

allows you to order demographic information by zip code. Pricing is by subscription, or information can be priced per requested report. Log on to www.infods.com for a free sample of reports and a free zip code search.

- **FedStats.** This Web site, at www.fedstats.gov, lets you track economic and population trends. The statistics are collected by more than 70 federal agencies.

- **Service Annual Survey.** This part of the U.S. Census' Web site offers annual estimates of receipts for some service industries. This information can be found at www.census.gov/svsd/www/sas.html.

- **Statistical Abstract of the U.S. Section 27, Domestic Trade and Services.** This Web page, located at www.census.gov/prod/2001pubs/ statab/sec27.pdf, provides information on sales employees, payrolls and other business statistics.

- **Statistical Resources on the Web.** This Web site, located at www.lib.umich.edu/govdocs/stats.html, is an index to statistical information available on the Web. It lists over 200 topics.

- **Statistics of Income.** Hosted by the Internal Revenue Service, this site contains financial information concerning businesses in the retail and service industries. You can find it by logging on to www.irs.gov/taxstats/display/0,,i1=40&genericId= 16810,00.html.

- **U.S. Department of Commerce's U.S. Bureau of Economic Analysis.** This agency hosts a Web site at www.bea.gov and provides publications and data on businesses by industry.

- **Define your competition.** Get as much information as you can about your competition. Establish what they're doing – successfully. Call a cross-section of caterers in the phone book. Ask them to mail you a copy of their menus. Try to find out, indirectly, what types of events they specialize in and which clients they have hosted recently.

- **Go to catered events whenever possible.** If there is an art show opening or fund-raiser, try to go. By attending events that are catered, you can learn about your competition and about potential events for your own business.

- **Talk to caterers.** In general, the food industry is pretty competitive, but if you are not in direct competition with a particular catering operation, the owner or manager may be willing to be interviewed and would be an excellent source of information.

- **Other sources of information on competition include the following ideas:**
  - **Telephone book.** You can at least get a count and the location of your competitors.

  - **Chambers of commerce.** These often keep a list of area businesses. Be careful using this list, however, it often only includes businesses that are members rather than all the businesses in the area.

  - **Trade magazines** can be sources of competitor information, especially if there are regional trade magazines.

  - **The U.S. Census Bureau** will have minimal information on businesses in the area. This information includes the number of businesses and number of employees.

- **Local newspapers.** You can get a sense of the competition from advertisements and job classifieds. Most papers also have a weekly entertainment section that lists a number of the restaurants in town with information on their prices and menus.

- **National Restaurant Association.** You can find a list by state of the number of establishments, projected sales and the number of employees they have at www.restaurant.org/research/state_st.cfm.

Define Your Customer

Apart from defining your market, you also need to define your customer profile. Will you, for example, be targeting wedding business or corporate catering? Will you focus on haute cuisine or food that is more homey and every-day? Here are some suggestions on how to gather information to draw your customer profile.

- **Interview potential customers.** Once you have a concept and target market in mind, interview people who are likely to become your customers. These people may be friends, or people that live in particular neighborhoods.

- **Trade magazines.** Trade magazines such as *Restaurant Hospitality* and *Restaurant and Institutions* are good sources for general customer information. *Restaurant Hospitality* can be found at www.restauranthospitality.com and *Restaurant and Institutions* is located at www.rimag.com.

- **There are also Web sites and magazines targeted specifically to the catering industry.** The site www.catersource.com is one such site. It offers business support for caterers including their online, bimonthly *CaterSource Journal.* A new magazine also can be found at www.cateringmagazine.com, a magazine published for professional caterers.

- **National Restaurant Association.** The National Restaurant Association also can provide you with some customer research. You can log onto the association's Web site at www.restaurant.org.

- **Visit www.marketreasearch.com.** This Web site has market research for the restaurant industry available for downloading. Costs run anywhere from $200 to several thousand dollars for reports that include titles such as "Fast Food in the USA," "Dining Out Market Review" and "Top Market Share Sandwich," "Pizza and Chicken Chain Restaurants Survey."

Business Plan and Market Analysis

As a part of your business plan, you need to write the market analysis portion of your plan. This section of the plan should describe your typical customer, define your target market, how you will advertise to promote your business, your pricing strategy and thoughts on the likelihood of growth and expansion. Don't have one yet? Get busy and write one, or hire a consultant to do it for you. There are many sources to consult when writing your business plan. This is an extremely important document for your business, so don't just wing it; get some expert advice (and use it!):

- **Small Business Administration (SBA).** The SBA offers "Resource Directory for Small Business Management" which includes a wealth of information, including how to write business plans. For a free copy, contact your nearest SBA office or log on to www.sba.gov.

- **Service Corps of Retired Executives (SCORE).** SCORE offers workshops and free counseling.

- **Business Information Centers (BIC).** These centers offer resources and on-site counseling for businesses. For more information about SBA business development programs and services, call the SBA Small Business Answer Desk at 800-U-ASK-SBA (827-5722), or log on to www.sba.gov/bi/bics.

- **U.S. Government Resources.** The Government Printing Office (GPO) offers resources to business owners as well. GPO bookstores are located in 24 major cities and listed in the Yellow Pages under the "bookstore" heading. You can write to Government Printing Office, Superintendent of Documents, Washington, D.C. 20402-9328 to request a list of materials they publish or you can purchase items from the bookstore online at bookstore.gpo.gov.

- **Atlantic Publishing** has publications that can help you write a business plan, www.atlantic-pub.com.

Marketing Your Business Plan

Marketing your business plan (and your fine reputation!) is especially important in the beginning. Don't cut corners. Invest in quality advertising for your establishment. Make sure that you spend every marketing buck effectively and productively. Remember, also, that your compensation will not always come in the form of dollars and cents – reputation is equally as valuable, perhaps more so in the long run. Here are a few more useful tips:

- **Be sensitive to your clients' needs.** Understand that when you market your business, you should keep in mind why your clients are buying catering services from you. Many of your clients who demand elaborate cuisine want to compete with their friends and relatives. They want to show that they can afford the luxury of hiring your catering services. Market your service in such a way as to satisfy their vanity.

- **Indirect marketing.** Those little personal touches that ooze "quality service" are in themselves your best form of marketing. A satisfied client is likely to pass on, by word of mouth, what superb service they've received. Make every effort to go that one step further to satisfy each and every client. It will certainly pay dividends in the long-term. For instance, if you are working as a home chef, prepare some breakfast muffins to leave for your client as an extra treat.

- **Weddings.** If you're interested in catering for weddings, you may want to contact florists, department store heads, musicians and personnel in charge of venues that book weddings. You also could list your company on Web sites set up for people planning weddings. At www.usabride.com and www.wedfind.com, you can be included in their list of local vendors.

- **Corporate catering?** Contact all corporations in your area, big and small. The chamber of commerce should be able to supply you with a list of local names. Bear in mind, also, that corporate clients buy first and foremost out of necessity and convenience.

- **Networking.** Join and become active in certain groups such as chambers of commerce, civic clubs (Rotary, Lions, Elks), church and synagogue groups, special-interest groups, NACE, NCA, etc. But remember, you're not asking them to buy catering, you're goal is to establish relationships with these people first. When they're ready to buy, they'll contact YOU. You can contact the NACE (National Association of Catering Executives) at www.nace.org. The NACE also offers a certification program, Achievement of the Certified Professional Catering

Executive (CPCE) designation, which would be a good marketing device.

- **Investigate the possibilities of "cause-related" marketing.** It allows you to help charitable organizations within your community while, at the same time, reaping the rewards from the publicity surrounding these charitable events. Every city has public radio fund drives, fundraising walks and other similar events. Consider providing lunch for the phone volunteers or setting up a booth with snacks for the walkers at the next event in your town.

- **Establish a connection with a community-service organization.** Galvanize positive public perception about your business. For instance, you may want to work with a local homeless group to organize a used-clothing drive. Enlist customers and employees to take part in walk-a-thons. Donate your restaurant's space and staff for a charity fund-raiser, etc. Network your restaurant's good deeds through your contacts in the community – the chamber of commerce, local clergy, alumni organizations or other civic groups.

- **When deciding which media to target, don't neglect small weekly papers.** Such newspapers might be hungrier for stories than major publications or television stations. Prepare a press release, along the lines outlined above, once you've determined which media to contact.

- **Work with the media.** Call newspapers to find out who the business or food restaurant reporters are and the best times to call. Next, call the appropriate person – at the appropriate time. Be brief, friendly and to the point. Don't mention that your business advertises in the newspaper, because editors don't run stories to help advertisers. Don't send gifts to editors or reporters, because they may see it as a form of bribery. Don't become hostile and never repeat a negative accusation made against your business.

- **Web marketing.** There are several online sources for marketing your catering business. Three of these sites are: www.leadingcaterers.com, www.localcatering.com, and partyleads.com. You can list your catering service on these sites and bid on business.

Marketing Tools

Although a good party goes a long way toward garnering new customers, using the right marketing tools can make a big difference to increasing your business. Reach your target market with press releases, media placement, mail campaigns and telephone solicitation. A Web site is also a must for any catering business today. Very few firms have the budget to spend large amounts of money on advertising, whether in local periodicals, on billboards or in other media. Thus, you must make use of marketing approaches that are innovative – and less costly. Many marketing concepts exist that can be implemented for a minimum of expense. In addition, a certain amount of ongoing investment in advertising is necessary, in order to give your business the best possible exposure in the local marketplace. Consider the following marketing tools:

- **Start with your portfolio.** Purchase a high-quality camera and take shots of every unique or distinctive event that you host. You may even find a staff member whose hobby is photography. Pay him or her to do the work for you. Photos should show your staff in uniform, some of your food displays and guests munching away enthusiastically. Select your best photos to use in brochures or mailings. Develop a set of catalogues. Catalogues should include bios of your chef and management team, along with a selection of your showpiece menus. Letters of recommendation are also good additions. But, be careful not to make the portfolio appear overwhelming.

- **Many caterers rely heavily on brochures.** A first-class brochure should include color photos and enticing text. Establish credibility by first telling your readers about the number of years in business, prominent clients, awards received, etc. Include information about your food and services and offer a guarantee for your services. Make your brochure easy to read. Deliver the message in as few words as possible.

- **Business cards and direct-mail campaigns still bring in customers.** Mail fliers to nearby corporate offices. Check periodically with the local chamber of commerce for updated business listings. Business cards and stationery should reflect the caterers' image. Get staff to carry business cards in their uniform shirt or jacket pocket so that they can retrieve them quickly. With regard to direct mail, include your catering menus, brochures, newsletters and other promotional literature to prospective clients in a little wallet with your logo on the cover.

- **Word of mouth.** By far the most important marketing tool you will need to cultivate is word of mouth. The key to developing leads is through connections. Whenever you do a large or distinctive function for a trade or business group, send an account of the event to the associated trade publications, along with photos. If the client is happy with your event, you should try to get a few good words of recommendation as well. In some cases you might want to ask if you can use their words of reference in your sales catalogues or brochures. Most brides, corporations, etc., are not going to risk embarrassment by trying an unknown caterer. In fact, many caterers' complete marketing plans are based on the favorable feedback of satisfied clients and guests. Other caterers know that they are only as good as their last party – and so do you.

- **Write effective press releases.** Write at least six press releases per year. Read the local newspapers and listen to local radio stations to get a feel for what they cover. Keep it short and to the point. Place the most important information at the beginning of the press release – and make sure your message is clear. Top the release with a headline that summarizes the story. Include photos of the event. Think of yourself as a reporter for the media when writing the press release; be objective. Give the who, what, when, where, why and how. A great resource to help you with press releases and ad copy is at www.wedding-andeventmarketing.com. You can download a publication entitled "How to Write Catering Ads that Sell" which gives tips on how to write sales and advertising copy. The site also offers a Wedding and Event Business Builder Toolkit Home Study Course, 561-776-1603, which costs about $800.

- **Signs, logos and names.** Pay for signs and logos that are large enough and that are easily seen, in addition to being professional. You may consider using your own name as part of your company name. If you do, you need not file a fictitious business name statement with your locality.

- **Tasting session.** Consider offering your prospective clients a sample of your food. The main advantage is that once caterers actually sit down with prospective clients and spend time discussing the menu, they know that they're significantly increasing their chances of gaining the business.

- **Cooking classes.** Another possible marketing tool is to offer cooking classes. You may be interested in doing a class at your facility, or just doing a demo at a mall kiosk to increase your public exposure.

The Internet and E-Commerce

The Internet opens up a whole new area of opportunity on the national and international catering market. A Web site is a powerful marketing tool. The Web is often the first place that people look when searching for particular products or services. An increasing number of potential clients, nowadays, use the Internet to make their initial inquiries. Your Web site, in effect, can act as an introduction to your services:

- **Engage a professional designer and copywriter to create your Web site.** It's clearly a necessity in today's market to have a Web presence. Bear in mind that a professional will be able to structure the site in such a way as to maximize on the number of "hits" your site achieves. Web sites can be put together with minimal expense and can provide tremendous impact and exposure. It's certainly the simplest and most efficient method of communicating with your potential customers. See www.gizwebs.com. Gizmo Graphics specializes in the food service area and will develop a low-cost, custom-designed Web site that will allow you to advertise, generate revenue, attract clients, promote your business and increase sales and revenue.

- **By including a broad portfolio on your Web site, you can feature the best of your efforts.** It never hurts to include numerous shots of your guests enjoying themselves as well. A picture, in this case, could mean a thousand dollars.

- **Wanna play big?** On a bigger scale, e-markets are rapidly emerging as the de facto standard for business-to-business e-commerce. The Internet is spawning new e-markets at a breakneck pace. By 2003, it is expected that 30-50 percent of all online B2B transactions will be channeled through these markets. For instance, with the help of Oracle

Corp. and Andersen Consulting, Catering Exchange, Inc., www.cateringx.com, has set up the world's first virtual marketplace, or "Internet exchange," focusing on the catering industry. CateringX already counts around 200 suppliers and buyers. Consider joining this virtual catering marketplace – now.

- **Compete with the "bigs."** With the Internet exchange, size doesn't matter anymore. Anyone who wants to compete with bigger companies can do so on the virtual exchange. For buyers, the exchange means lower prices and big savings. For example, CateringX publishes in its online catalogue, 50 "units" or products for each supplier – free of charge. It expects to earn commissions from every transaction made on the site; the site would charge around a 2-percent service fee from each transaction made on the site.

Sales and Closing the Sale

Selling runs parallel to marketing and both are essential to the continued success of your catering operation. However, before deciding on your overall sales strategy, you'll first need to focus closely upon your target audience. Decide where you're going pitch your market. In other words, locate your clients and establish the types of clients with whom you'd like to work. There's nothing less rewarding than working with an impossible client. Try the following approach:

- **Start qualifying your clients immediately.** Some clients ease up when they see that they can trust you, but some will never soften up. Don't waste your time with the second type of clients.

- **Payment.** Try to establish quickly (and, of course, discreetly) whether the client has sufficient funds to pay for your services. Aim to qualify them right away. If their budget still remains questionable, send them to your competition. Be suspicious when the promised deposits are not sent to you. If you already have a heavy commitment during the time of a proposed event, refuse, no matter how good a client is. Do not over-commit yourself and your staff.

- **Segment.** If you're targeting several markets at once, it makes sense to segment your marketing strategies and/or staff. Many firms divide their sales staff by corporate or private catering, or even by specific types of functions, such as weddings, receptions, dinners or special entertainment-related events. Develop specialist staff. Let them focus on a specific area, thus gaining greater expertise and familiarity with all the particulars of their assignment.

- **Specialize.** At what types of events are you best? Where is your competitive advantage over the competition? For example, if you can't handle large functions profitably (in the 500-person range, say), then you may want to eliminate these clients from your target list. On the other hand, if your business has the facilities and expertise to put on elegant wedding receptions, then that segment of the market should be targeted for an appropriate amount of sales resources.

- **Develop and manage leads.** All your analysis and strategizing must, ultimately, be turned into something tangible and money-producing. The first step in closing a sale is generating a lead. Remember, the most successful salespeople are those who develop and pursue leads, aggressively. This is an area where sheer volume pays off. Set up a client database, containing not just names and addresses, but any information you can dig up, including every contact you have had with the potential customer. Include any miscellaneous comments that a salesperson might feel is relevant to a future sale.

- **Your goal is to expand your client list.** This can be achieved through lead referrals, advertising and – sometimes – aggressive cold calling. Work your leads like your job depended on it (as, of course, it does). The most successful salespeople are not the ones with the flashiest smiles, or most elegant presentations, but simply the ones who are the most persistent. Pay close attention to which conventions and groups are coming to town, as far in advance as you can gather the information.

- **Use your current bookings to develop new ones.** One of the keys to developing leads is through networking your existing contacts. If the client is happy with your event, then you should try to get a few good words of recommendation as well. In some cases you might want to ask if you may use their words of reference in your sales catalogues or brochures. Be sure to add all influential attendees of your functions to your database.

- **"Follow-up."** There's nothing wrong with a follow-up correspondence with someone who may have just been introduced to you at a banquet that you're hosting. You should make it hard for your customers to forget that you want their business and you appreciate it. In addition, make them reluctant to contract with another caterer. The most important asset any company has is its reputation. Protect it and promote it vigorously.

General Pricing Considerations

Every catering event is a negotiation and a relationship. In order to make the most of your pricing potential, you first have to find out exactly what's important to your client. Regardless of the rate, a great deal of planning is required. A caterer is only as good as the information that he or she is able to obtain from the client. Without happy clients, there is no catering business. To ensure that both the caterer and the client are satisfied, good communication is essential throughout the entire process. Consider the following issues when trying to arrive at a price that is acceptable both to you, the caterer, and to your client:

- **What should be included in a "per-person" charge?** Don't forget that per-person charges also cover the cost of room rental. Clients don't like to see this as a line item, so work it into your overall costs instead. Alcoholic beverages, however, are not normally included. Customers are usually required to pay on a consumption basis, with the options of an open or cash bar and house or premium brand spirits at different price points. Additional supplies should be billed as line items. Standard linens are part of the per-person price, but themed linens are extra. The same goes for chair covers and other amenities.

- **Factor all additional costs into the billing.** On top of the pricing decisions regarding rentals, markups, service charges, discounts and more, caterers serving off-premise events encounter a host of additional costs. Don't forget to factor these costs into their billing. Transportation costs, for example, include more than just vehicle purchase or rental. They also involve additional expenses such as gasoline, parking, tolls, insurance and even parking tickets or towing fees. Disposables, such as plastic wrap to cover pans, detergent for washing dishes, boxes, aluminum foil, plastic gloves and hand wipes, are another often-overlooked expense.

- **For more elaborate off-premise events, caterers may even add an extra charge.** Certain events may warrant an additional charge. Take as an example, the hosting of a tent party in Chicago in October or an event on a boat in the middle of a lake that requires more labor than a simple indoor banquet. Bill unusual events accordingly.

- **Place settings and pricing.** Never set a single setting more than the client has agreed to pay for. Remember that your service staff assignments and your kitchen are all tied into the set count. Just because you set a few extra tables doesn't mean the kitchen will have meals prepared, or, for that matter, that you'll have staff to service them. It will, however, give the client that impression. All clients have a vested interest in keeping the guarantee count as close to the actual count as possible. They will "nickel and dime" you to death with set changes, if you don't establish firm rules.

- **Finalizing the deal.** Once prices have been agreed, ask your client to check and finalize the details of the event. Also, at this point, ask the client to sign off on the number of people to be served and the specific quantities of food and beverages you've agreed upon. This is your contract.

- **Guarantee.** Base the guarantee on the number of guests that the client has agreed to pay for – regardless of how many people actually eat. The contract generally covers a certain cushion beyond the guarantee (often 5 percent), which the caterer agrees to set and prepare for in the event that a few extra show up. Some caterers specify that any amendments to the guarantee, within 24 hours, automatically changes the guarantee count to the set count and that the client will be billed accordingly.

- **Gratuities.** Some caterers add gratuities for servers into the invoice and others don't. In general, gratuities are usually 15-25 percent of the total food and beverage cost.

Pricing Guidelines

The "per-person" rate of some caterers includes all or most of their costs, from food and beverages to china and table linens. Others restrict per-person fees to food and beverages alone, choosing to bill other expenses as individual line items, each with its own profit margin. Regardless of their method, however, caterers share a familiar goal: to recoup costs with enough left over for a reasonable profit. The art of pricing is to charge enough to earn an overall profit, but not so much that most proposals are lost.

- **Typical charges for a catering event.** Caterers usually charge per person for an event. Rates vary considerably and are based on the type of event and food. For a luncheon, a price between $8 and $12 is an average range. Dinners may fall as low as $9, but they may also run as high as $75 per person. A caterer knows what their overhead costs and "break-even" figures are. In order to make a living, the caterer must charge more than this figure. Logically then, the greater the number, the bigger the profit. This is why many large reception facilities have a "minimum" policy. For example, a facility may have determined it will take a minimum of 250 guests at $15 per person to meet overhead expenses and to allow for a modest profit.

- **Pricing buffets and receptions.** Charge either by the guest count or by the piece. Charging by the piece means you agree to provide and set out a specific quantity of specified items. If the client decides they need, or want, more, then bill them for these additions. Be prepared. Ask the chef, in advance, for a list of items available for replenishment in case the client decides to reorder. Of course, if you have a backup ready and it is not needed, you will be wasting some money on food cost because you cannot pass this charge for backup supplies on to the customer.

- **Pricing a meal buffet.** For buffets, clients are generally charged "per person." A plate count should be taken before and after the function to determine the number actually served. Meal buffets often have a guarantee and a set count, billed in the same manner as a seated function.

- **What do you do if a client tries to negotiate a reduction?** Frequently, you'll be asked to reduce quoted prices. A good philosophy is not to reduce a price without reducing something else in the event. You can work with a client who wants a reduction. To accomplish this, you may need to discuss limiting the buffet to two entrée choices rather than three, or perhaps switching out the seafood entrée for a less-expensive item, such as chicken.

- **As a general approach to pricing a catering event, you may wish to consider the following guidelines:**
  - First, determine how much your competitors charge for the same services.

  - Second, determine your costs for producing the food items.

  - Use the total cost of all your raw materials for a particular recipe, to calculate your overhead and labor cost.

  - Add up a year's total cost (not including food and related expenses), like rent, insurance, business taxes, utilities, depreciation, etc. From this total your derive your daily overhead expense.

  - Calculate your labor costs in the same way.

  - "Shortcut" pricing method. You can always use the other much easier method: simply multiply the material cost by three. The figure you arrive at, however, still needs to be modified. For example, depending on the preparation time for a specific food, you may need to multiply your raw material cost by four, not three, in some circumstances.

CHAPTER TEN

BUDGETING & ACCOUNTING

Accounting Systems

An understanding of your own budget (along with the client's) will help you to devise menu plans that will keep everyone happy and your operation profitable. Planning and pulling off a beautiful and elaborate banquet that impresses everyone, but loses money, will be your showpiece only for a little while. Ultimately, it is profitability that will be the measure of your success. Here are a few record-keeping tips that will help you make a profit:

- **Get Computerized**. The reality is, no matter what type or size of your food service operation, our advice is get your operation computerized. It's extremely difficult to compete successfully without utilizing technology, at least to some degree. Today the investment for a basic computer and accounting software is less than $2,000 and could be as little as $1,000. The investment will deliver immediate savings in accounting fees and your ability to get true insight into your business.

- **QuickBooks.** Our favorite restaurant accounting package, without a doubt, is the veteran QuickBooks® by Intuit. The QuickBooks' 2002 version is rich in features, including built-in remote-access capabilities and Web interfaces. Reports are generated in a few seconds that would take hours to calculate manually. The reports are also flawless, eliminating the human-error factor. This program now has a POS option that was the only limiting factor prior to this new release. QuickBooks is available at www.quickbooks.com. Another popular accounting package is Peachtree, available at www.peachtree.com.

- **Tasty Profits software.** If you are just setting up your accounting program and decide to use QuickBooks®, we recommend an add-on product called "The Tasty Profits Guide to QuickBooks® Software for Restaurants." This helpful guide to QuickBooks® enables you to save thousands of dollars doing your own accounting with its proven, easy-to-use system. Simply install the floppy disc that is included with the "Tasty Profits Guide" directly into your computer, download the pre-configured restaurant accounts and you are ready to go. You will have instant access to all your financial data; calculate accurate food and bar costs with ease; reconcile bank and credit card statements; track and pay tips that are charged to credit cards; and calculate sales tax automatically. The program costs about $70 and is available at www.atlantic-pub.com, 800-541-1336, Item TP-01.

Chart of Accounts

Restaurant accounting requires specific procedures. Concentrate on the essentials. The following suggestions will point you in the right direction:

- **The Uniform System of Accounts for Restaurants (USAR).** The National Restaurant Association publishes a simple, easy-to-use accounting classification system for restaurants. This valuable book, prepared by CPAs, includes examples of balance sheets, wage-control reports and an expense-classification system. If you take only one idea from this book, we recommend you use this system. You can order on line at www.restaurant.org, or by calling 800-424-5156. USAR is an essential guide for restaurant accounting. It establishes a common industry language that allows you to compare ratios and percentages across industry lines. The goal of this comparison is to create financial statements that are management tools, not just IRS reports.

- **Accounts used for recording revenues and expenses may include the following:**

Revenue accounts:
- Food revenues
- Mixers, bar setup revenue
- Equipment revenue
- Floral and décor revenue
- Music and entertainment revenue
- Revenues from other services
- Sales tax collected

Expense revenues (Cost of Sales Accounts):
- Cost of sales - food
- Cost of sales - mixers, setups
- Cost of sales - equipment
- Cost of sales - floral and décor
- Cost of sales - music and entertainment
- Cost of sales - other services

Payroll and related costs (Direct Operating Costs):
- Uniforms
- Laundry
- Replacement costs
- Supplies
- Transportation
- Licenses and permits
- Miscellaneous
- Advertising and promotion
- Utilities
- Sales tax reimbursement to state

Administrative and general expenses:

- Office supplies, printing and postage
- Telephone
- Data processing costs
- Dues and subscriptions
- Insurance
- Fees to credit organizations
- Professional fees
- Repairs and maintenance
- Rent and lease expense

Grasp the Basics of Budgeting

The successful caterers will always be those who can balance the sale of the event with its cost. It's as simple as that. Accountancy procedures, however, can sometimes appear daunting to the uninitiated. So, here are a few explanations that will help you get to grips with the basics of budgeting and accounting:

- **It is important for caterers to understand that records must be kept on a daily basis.** Record revenues and expenses immediately. Don't make the mistake of not keeping your records up to date. There can be government penalties if you fall behind with your accounts.

- **Taxes on money received.** A popular method for many small businesses is that of not paying taxes on money received until the following tax year. In 1987 however, the Congress closed this loophole. Small businesses are now obliged to use cash-accounting on a calendar basis. So unless your accountant devises some means of circumvention, you'll have to declare all income when you receive it. You'll also have to deduct expenses when you pay them. At the same time, the "tax" year for your business will be the same as your "personal" tax year.

- **Cash versus accrual-basis accounting.** The latter accounts for income and expenses, according to the job to which they are allocated – and not as these expenses are paid for or received. With an accrual-based system, for example, you are able to shift out a deposit and if your event is postponed/cancelled more than, say, 10 days before January 14, you could still get your money back. You won't have to bear the tax expense on your deposit either.

- **Gross versus Net Profit.** Get to grips with this one – it's a very important accounting concept! Your Gross Profit is what you make on an event after paying the expenses allocated specifically to that event. When you deduct the operating costs from the Gross Profit, you get the Net Profit Before Tax.

- **Overheads.** It is vital to know what the overheads are for your business; e.g., rent, equipment lease payments, labor costs, insurance, purchased equipment, etc. Calculating a "pro rata" share of overhead can be done in one of two ways. Note, however, that these methods assume regular future business and do not necessarily take into account your start-up costs:

- **The first calculation is calendar based:** Add up your entire overheads for the year (including your taxes and your living expenses). Divide the total by twelve.

- **The second method is a dollar percentage:** Add to each dollar of direct-event expense, a markup percentage that includes your margin for overheads, plus taxes, plus net profit.

- **Certified Public Accounts.** Tip: Your accounting system does not replace Certified Public Accountants (CPA). It only provides you with figures that will enable you to manage your business more effectively.

- **Assets.** Assets include cash, accounts receivable, inventory, buildings and equipment. Consider a tactic called factoring where the caterer "sells" his or her current debts (Accounts Receivable) to a collection agency in return for cash.

Income Statement and Balance Sheet

The income statement and balance sheet show the financial status of your business. The income statement shows the Net Profit (or Loss) for a certain accounting period. The balance sheet, on the other hand, is a snapshot of the financial health of your business operations on a given date. It depicts the assets and liabilities, as well as the Net Worth of your company, which is exactly the figure you get if you deduct total liabilities from total assets. You'll need to understand the basics about calculating your income statement. Start with the following:

- **First, understand the terminology.**

- **What are Operating Revenues?** Operating Revenues are payments received from clients.

- **What are Operating Expenses?** Operating Expenses represent running costs; e.g., wages and salaries.

- **What are Expenses Incurred?** These expenses represent the cost of goods used to serve the client.

- **Here is the basic formula for calculating an Income Statement:**

    Operating revenue - operating expenses = net income/loss

If you subtract the Operating Revenue from the Sales, you arrive at Gross Margin.

- **The balance sheet.** Concentrate on the four important factors that affect your balance sheet:
  - The personal investment you have made in the business.
  - Your ability to obtain credit or borrowed capital.
  - Your ability to compete in the market.
  - The location (as well as local economic conditions) of the place where your business operates.

- **A balance bheet, in general, has three main categories:**
  - **Assets:** what your business owns.
  - **Liabilities:** what your business owes its creditors.
  - **Equity:** your market value, on a given date – either historical or projected. Owner's equity is the amount of money invested by the owner to set up the business.

Understanding Cash Flow

Fact: Businesses fail due to poor cash flow management. Why? First, you need to understand the implications of ready cash and day-to-day cash-flow management. Remember, ready cash means actual money in the bank, or in the business. It does not mean inventory, accounts receivable or property. Granted, the latter can be converted to cash, at some point in time, but we're talking here about cash on hand – the ready cash needed to pay the rent and meet the payroll, etc. Profit, on the other hand, is the amount of money you expect to make if all customers pay on time and your expenses are spread out evenly over the time period being measured. It is not your day-to-day reality. The bottom line is that you must have cash in order to keep the doors of your business open while juggling long-term profitability and the minutiae of running a busy catering operation. Learn the basics about how to manage your cash flow. It can mean the difference between the success and failure of your catering operation:

- **Cash Flow.** This term refers to the flow of cash in and out of a business over a certain period of time. If the cash coming "in" to the business is more than the cash going "out" of the business, your company has a positive cash flow. If the opposite is the case, consider, possibly, selling obsolete inventory to redress the cash flow imbalance.

- **The Annual Cash Flow Projection.** This should be on the "must do" list for all small businesses. In fact, most equity investors or lenders will want you to show them a long-term cash flow projection. So, how do you set about preparing a cash flow projection?

- **Start the projection with budgeted Net Profit or Loss** and then adjust for non-cash items, such as depreciation expense.

- **Next, adjust for timing differences** (insurance premiums, property taxes charged to expenses each month, but paid once per year). It is important, at this stage, to make sure that your income statement, balance sheet and statement of cash flows reconcile, if you're preparing projections for a loan package or other financing.

- **Strategic statement of cash flows are prepared on either a quarterly or annual basis.** For example, you may want to include a monthly cash flow projection for year 1, quarterly projections for years 2 and 3 and annual projections for years 4 and 5. It is best to follow the format of separating operating cash flow from investing and financing activities.

- **Operating Cash Flow.** Often referred to as working

capital, this refers to the cash generated from the sales of your catering services, the lifeblood of your business.

- **Investing Cash Flow.** This is generated, internally, from non-operating activities. It includes investments in plant and equipment or other fixed assets, or other sources.

- **Financing Cash Flow.** This refers to the cash flow to and from external sources; e.g., lenders, investors and shareholders. Include new loans, the repayment of loans, issuance of stock and dividends in this section of your statement of cash flows.

- **The longer the period allowed for your clients to pay their bills, the more your cash flow will suffer.** Take a lesson from the past. Many years ago, it was common practice to invoice the client for the food and services 2-4 weeks after the event. As corporate catering grew, many caterers' payment policies evolved to accommodate their clients' financial payment policies. These clients would disburse their final payment between 45 and 90 days after the event. If you want to avoid such cash-flow problems, be a smart caterer; create a formal, written payment policy based on the financial needs and the mission of your catering operation.

- **Payment policy.** Request payment from the client of one-third of the total bill at the point when the contract is signed, with the next third due immediately before or on the day of the event and the final third due within 30 days after the event. This type of payment schedule is flexible and could be adapted depending upon the type of function and the client.

- **Other factors affecting your cash flow are**

separate income and expense budgets. Take, for example, prepaid expenses, such as insurance and utility deposits. Payroll costs are generally paid within one week of the party date and their effect on cash flow should be minimal.

Financing and Keeping Track of Money

In order to acquire funds from external sources to finance your business activities and to monitor and control those funds effectively, it is vital that you're able to forecast the short- and long-term financial needs of your operation. It is impossible to over-emphasize the important role played by accurate forecasting in the long-term sustainability of your business. It is crucial for you and your business. In order to create a healthy balance between risk and profitability, you must first establish sound financial management procedures. You'll also need to understand and apply the principles of successful capital raising, relationship-building with the capital-suppliers, the implications of credit policy and the need for a complete accounting and budgeting system. Your ability, as a caterer, to secure funds from financial markets, will depend, largely upon how long you've been in business; i.e., whether it is less than a year, or more than a year. Consider the following important issues when seeking funding or financing for your catering operation:

- **Explore all sources of financing first.** Before seeking external sources of capital, you should explore, thoroughly, all reasonable sources for meeting your capital needs internally. Even if this effort fails to generate all of the needed capital, it can significantly reduce the burden of external financing requirements. Internal investment means less interest expense, lower repayment obligations and less sacrifice of control. What's more – your ability to generate maximum capital internally and to control operations will enhance the confidence of outside investors and lenders. The knock-on effect? Outside finance companies will be more willing to commit their capital to your operation.

- **Equity financing.** Explore the possibilities of equity financing, via raising funds through the issue of stock, retained earnings or funds generated from depreciation. Unlike debt, equity capital is permanently invested in the business. You have no legal obligation for repayment of the amount invested or for payment of interest for the use of the funds. The equity investor basically shares in the ownership of the business and is entitled to participate in any distribution of earnings through dividends. Bear in mind that the extent of participation is in proportion to the number of shares held.

- **Liability of the equity investor.** Liability is limited to the amount of their investment in a corporation. It is not set against any personal assets held by the investor. Typically, your equity investor will expect to be compensated for his or her investment either in the form of income from earnings distribution (dividends paid out to shareholders) or as capital gains (realized upon the sale of the business), or from selling his or her interest shares to other partners.

- **Please understand that your equity investor is assuming substantial risk.** In fact, unlike the secured creditor, he or she has no specific claim against any assets of your business. Only after all claims of all creditors are satisfied in liquidation, are the remaining assets made available for distribution. Even then, the equity investor's participation in the proceeds is restricted to a share proportionate to the number of shares held. This is the reason that equity investors, in the case of small businesses, generally expect a considerably higher return on investment than the lender – perhaps 20-50 percent, or even more.

- **Debt financing.** Beware! This is money borrowed that will have to be paid back within a definite payment schedule and by a due date. Worse, in most cases, it has to be paid back at a hefty rate of interest. So, look to the banks where you keep your general, payroll and checking accounts. Understand that banks have some pretty conservative lending practices, so you should try to establish a relationship. Provide them with the financial statements showing realistic and accurate figures. Be prepared to answer detailed bankers' inquiries about your statement.

- **Bank loans.** Banks usually consider several factors when making loan determinations. These may include:
  - How long you've been in operation.
  - The nature of your business.
  - Your individual character.
  - Your capacity to repay, if the capital loans are guaranteed by the owner.
  - The existence of collateral; e.g. your personal property (which, incidentally could be seized if you don't pay back the loan).
  - The existence of home equity, personal savings accounts, etc.

- **SBA-guaranteed loans.** Consider the possibility of taking out an SBA-guaranteed loan. These loans are sometimes granted to entrepreneurs who do not qualify for commercial loans. They offer an extended payment schedule of between 7-8 years.

- **Keep borrowing to an absolute minimum.** Whatever type of funding you decide upon, the burden of repayment can seriously affect not only your day-to-day cash flow, but also the ultimate survival of your business. Remember that interest rates on loans can cripple even the most "successful" of catering businesses.

INDEX